"You need grit to get great, and this book succinctly tells you how to do it. There's no sugar coating: Kaplan Thaler and Koval tell it like it is, because they've used grit to achieve great success themselves. I recommend it."

—Mark Sanborn, bestselling author of *The Fred Factor*

"Kaplan Thaler and Koval have written a very valuable book. Their insights and anecdotes on the importance of hard work, perseverance, and character provide timeless lessons that will resonate with their readers, from the senior executive to the summer intern."

—Gail J. McGovern, president and CEO,
American Red Cross

"In *Grit to Great*, Linda Kaplan Thaler and Robin Koval remind us that it takes much more than a diploma or high pedigree to be successful. It takes equal parts hard work, determination, pluck, and willingness to confront adversity and failure head-on . . . *Grit to Great* is a celebratory tribute to the great American success story."

—Abraham H. Foxman, national director,
Anti-Defamation League

"In *Grit to Great*, Linda and Robin have written what is sure to be another bestseller. It's a simple, well-written, inspiring read that will get you going on your own journey from grit to great."

—Andrea March, cofounder, Women's Leadership Exchange

Grit to Great

Also by Linda Kaplan Thaler and Robin Koval

The Power of Small
The Power of Nice
Bang! Getting Your Message Heard in a Noisy World

Grit to Great

*How Perseverance, Passion, and Pluck
Take You from Ordinary to Extraordinary*

By Linda Kaplan Thaler
and Robin Koval

CROWN
BUSINESS
NEW YORK

Published in the United States by Crown Business,
an imprint of the Crown Publishing Group,
a division of Penguin Random House LLC, New York.
www.crownpublishing.com

CROWN BUSINESS is a trademark and CROWN and the Rising Sun
colophon are registered trademarks of Penguin Random House LLC.

Crown Business books are available at special discounts for bulk
purchases for sales promotions or corporate use. Special editions,
including personalized covers, excerpts of existing books, or books
with corporate logos, can be created in large quantities for special
needs. For more information, contact Premium Sales at (212) 572-
2232 or e-mail specialmarkets@penguinrandomhouse.com.

Library of Congress Cataloging-in-Publication Data
Kaplan Thaler, Linda.
    Grit to great : how perseverance, passion, and pluck take you from
ordinary to extraordinary / Linda Kaplan Thaler and Robin Koval.
— First edition.
        pages cm
1. Success. 2. Success in business. 3. Determination (Personality
trait) 4. Career development. I. Koval, Robin. II. Title.
    BF637.S8K346 2015
    650.1—dc23

                        2015021014

ISBN 978-0-8041-3912-0
eBook ISBN 978-0-8041-3913-7

PRINTED IN THE UNITED STATES OF AMERICA

Book design by Anna Thompson
Jacket design by Kalena Schoen
Jacket paint texture: Itsmesimon / Shutterstock
Jacket background texture: chrupka / Shutterstock

10 9 8 7 6 5 4 3 2 1

First Edition

For my loving parents, Bertha and Marvin,
for teaching me the value of hard work and perseverance.

LINDA KAPLAN THALER

In loving memory of my parents, Marilyn and Seymour—
the source and inspiration of my grit.
Thank you.

ROBIN KOVAL

Contents

CHAPTER 1

Why Grit Matters

The difference between a successful person and others is not a lack of strength, not a lack of knowledge, but rather a lack of will.

—VINCE LOMBARDI

STEVE JOBS. COLIN POWELL. MICHAEL JORDAN. ALL FA-mous individuals who excelled in their fields, and whose names have become synonymous with excellence and achievement. But apart from that you are probably unaware of any similarity between them. After all, what does one of the most transformational pioneers of the personal software industry have to do with leading troops into battle, or guiding America's foreign policy? And what do the exploits of the greatest basketball player of his generation have to do with Silicon Valley or the Pentagon? But these three over-achievers share one very surprising trait. All three were so ordinary growing up that virtually no one predicted their future greatness. They were all easily overlooked and dismissed, their talents grossly underestimated.

Steve Jobs had a 2.65 GPA in high school and never completed his first year of college. As a high school sophomore, Michael Jordan went home in tears after his basketball coach decided he wasn't good enough to make the cut for the school's varsity team. The future secretary of state and chairman of the US Joint Chiefs of Staff trudged through high school with a very ordinary C average, and scant self-confidence. Not long ago, Colin Powell told an interviewer, "I never thought I would be someone important. I was just a pretty average kid with average grades in an average home. There was nothing special about me."

So what was it that changed the course of Powell's life? How is it that countless successful people don't display obvious special gifts, talent, or genius early on? How do you catch up in the game of life when you aren't blessed with perfect scores on your SAT or an Ivy League education or a family fortune to give you a head start?

Emerging research suggests that there is far more to success in life than a country club pedigree or natural ability and sheer talent. Passion and perseverance, it turns out, matter more than talent or intelligence when it comes to being successful. For most of us, the corner office or professional kudos is the result of hard work, rather than exceptional genes. The endgame, it turns out, belongs to the truly diligent, not the merely talented. It belongs to those who have *grit*.

Grit is a somewhat old-fashioned term, resurrected from a previous century. But it is enjoying a remarkable renaissance these days. Why? Because it seems as if we are getting soft. Grit is about sweat, not swagger. Character, not charisma. Grit has been equated more with methodical stick-to-itiveness and survival than any secret ingredient to success. Which is too bad, because for so many, grit *is* the secret to success. Grit is the result of a hard-fought struggle, a willingness to take risks, a strong sense of determination, working relentlessly toward a goal, taking challenges in stride, and having the passion and perseverance to accomplish difficult things, even if you are wallowing in the most difficult circumstances.

Perhaps what *we* love most about grit is that you don't have to be born with it. It can be learned. In fact, perseverance and the value of hard work have been, since the time of the Greek philosophers, always considered to be core elements of raising and educating the next generation. Aristotle, writing about the virtues of hard work, said, "We are what we repeatedly do. Excellence then is not an act but a habit." Our Founding Fathers, with their great admiration for the classical philosophers, embraced these tenets. From the revolution to the westward expansion, through the industrial revolution, up through the end of World War II, the belief that raising strong, resilient, and self-reliant children was each parent's responsibility was part of our cultural DNA. But then something changed.

Don't Flatter Yourself

Since the late 1960s, two generations have been raised under the banner of the self-esteem movement, in which psychologists have told parents and educators that praise will give their children more confidence, which will help them be successful. At the height of the craze, the California legislature established a self-esteem task force for the state's schools and in 1989 issued a report that persuaded schools nationwide to nurture their students' self-esteem as a way of eliminating social problems and academic failure. But guess what—it hasn't worked.

The result has been that children get a trophy even when they lose. In some sports, coaches don't even keep score anymore. Grade inflation from elementary school through college has become a major issue, and although American students rank low on skills, they are at the top of the world in believing they're good at math. Millennials' sense of entitlement in the workplace, where twenty-somethings expect to be swiftly promoted even in their first jobs, has become the stuff of HR department lore. As have "fluffed up" performance reviews from supervisors afraid to give a little tough love to staff for fear of demoralizing them.

The fact that so many of us think we are exceptional has thoroughly permeated pop culture. As the main character in the 2004 children's movie *The Incredibles* said, "They keep inventing new ways to celebrate mediocrity." The seventh-place ribbons adorning the walls in *Meet the Fockers* were comedic, but not too far from the truth in our "everyone is special" culture.

Unfortunately, the whole self-esteem movement has been a flop, undermining the natural grit that this nation of immigrants brought with them in building a new life in a new land. And there is the beginning of a backlash.

You're Nothing Special

In his famous commencement speech, which quickly went viral, English teacher David McCullough Jr. told the Class of 2012 graduates of Wellesley High School (an affluent Boston suburb), "You're not special. . . . Contrary to what your U9 soccer trophy suggests, your glowing seventh-grade report card, despite every assurance of a certain corpulent purple dinosaur, that nice Mister Rogers and your batty aunt Sylvia, no matter how often your maternal caped crusader has swooped in to save you—you're nothing special." McCullough said Americans have "come to love accolades more than genuine achievement. No longer is it how you play the game, no longer is it even whether you win or lose, or learn or grow, or enjoy yourself doing it. Now it's 'So what does this get me?'" He urged the graduates to read, and concluded, "The fulfilling life, the distinctive life, the relevant life, is an achievement, not something that will fall into your lap because you're a nice person or Mommy ordered it from the caterer."

After reviewing fifteen thousand studies that the self-esteem movement generated, author Kay Hymowitz wrote in the *Los Angeles Times,* "High self-esteem doesn't improve grades, reduce anti-social behavior, deter alcohol drinking or do much of anything good for kids. In fact, telling kids how smart they are can be counterproductive. Many children who are convinced that they are little geniuses tend not to put much effort into their work. Others are troubled by the latent anxiety of adults who feel it necessary to praise them constantly."

In a 2012 study using eye tracking, researchers Bradley Morris and Shannon Zentall asked kids to draw pictures. Those who heard praise suggesting they had an innate talent—as opposed to those who were praised for their effort—were twice as fixated on mistakes they'd made in their pictures.

What this tells us is that children who are outperformed may give up rather than fight to improve, and those who do win may not feel compelled to keep trying as hard if even the losers get praise and a trophy.

Everyone could benefit from being taught to strive—the US Department of Education is now encouraging the teaching of grit and resilience among all students.

Meghan Dunn agrees. She is the founding principal of Riverdale Avenue Community School PS 446, located in Brownsville, Brooklyn. Many of her students are from low-income homes. She believes grit is their path to success. She instills grit by pushing her students out of their comfort zone—taking city kids camping, having them play chess or a team sport—and learning how to take losing in stride. She encourages students by teaching problem-solving skills, asking, "Well, what do you think?" or "What would you do?" She encourages parents and guardians to make sure that their kids finish whatever they start, even when it gets hard, and to let kids do things for themselves. She tells parents not to do the packing for those camping trips, because if they do, the students cannot find what they need and cannot figure out how to repack. To Meghan, forgetting a flashlight is not a life-or-death experience, but a teaching opportunity, so that when kids get older they know how to think and plan ahead. She believes it is the small things that teach kids grit—having chores and responsibilities, and an adult to offer support.

Bob Deutsch, a PhD in cognitive neuroscience, has a unique perspective on the role of grit in shaping our lives.

"There are different levels of grit," Deutsch told us. "It's not a unified, generic, all-or-nothing concept. There's a million people who have grit, and there's a million who don't. But of those who don't, at least eighty percent could have grit." In other words, it's a trait that can be developed, a skill that can be learned when a person is exposed to the right kind of training, experiences, and practice.

We would argue that it was grit that enabled "Air Jordan" to go on to dazzle his high school JV team and ultimately become, well, Michael Jordan. How does Jordan sum up what it took to become the best player in basketball history? "I've missed more than nine thousand shots in my career. I've lost almost three hundred games. Twenty-six times, I've been entrusted to take the game-winning shot and missed. I've failed over and over and over again in my life, and that's why I succeed."

For Colin Powell, the son of Jamaican immigrants, it wasn't until he attended the City College of New York that he found his calling—in the Reserve Officers Training Corps. ROTC gave him the structure he needed and he soon became commander of his unit, launching his historic career.

For Steve Jobs, getting fired in 1985 from Apple, the company he founded—and the failure of his subsequent venture, NeXT Computer—set the stage for one of the most remarkable business comebacks in history. As he confessed in his commencement speech at Stanford University, "[I]t turned out that getting fired from Apple was the best thing that could have ever happened to me. The heaviness of being successful was replaced by the lightness of being a beginner again, less sure about everything. It freed me to enter one of the most creative periods of my life."

Michael Bloomberg, the three-time mayor of New York City whose $30 billion fortune makes him one of the richest people in the world, summed up the essential concept of grit when he explained his secret to success in an interview with *New York* magazine.

"I know what hard work is all about," Bloomberg said. "I still come back to what my strategy always was and will continue to be: I'm not the smartest guy, but I can outwork you. It's the one thing I can control."

We feel the same way about grit and hard work ourselves.

Get a Bronx Attitude

We both grew up in the Bronx—a place that for generations has been synonymous with grit. We grew up in hardworking families of modest means.

Robin's father had a small taxi business; her mother was a bookkeeper. Her parents instilled the value of hard work in her from an early age. When Robin would get a grade of 96 percent, her mother would say, encouragingly, "Next time, get one hundred." Robin attended Syracuse University with the help of scholarships and work-study jobs. When her fine arts degree in graphic design failed to land her a dream job in the white-shoe boys' club of Madison Avenue, she learned to type and got an administrative job in an ad agency. She watched others around her advance as she typed—badly.

"Inspired, I went back to school for an MBA, determined to work my way up to that corner office I craved." And she did. Robin says, "While I may at times have resented that my achievements have come less easily than others', today it is one of the things I value most in my life."

Linda came from a middle-class family; her parents worked tirelessly to put food on the family table. Linda honed her comedic instincts and wit at that table, hoping for some of the adulation her brilliant brother received. Like the rest of her family, she attended the local public City College of New York, and then struggled as a teacher, performer, and songwriter for years, before finally landing a job in advertising. She spent the next seventeen years using her talent, tenacity, and perseverance to create notable campaigns and jingles for Kodak ("Kodak Moments"), Burger King, and Toys "R" Us, among others. Although Linda would agree her natural ability took her a couple of rungs up the ladder, it was her ability to bounce back after endless client rejections, and thousands of rewrites, that took her the rest of the way.

In 1997, Linda was the chief creative officer at a now-defunct New York ad agency and had been working on the Clairol business when another client asked her to resign Clairol because he felt it was in direct conflict with one of their hair care brands. With the backing of Clairol's then CEO, Steve Sadove, Linda decided to resign as well and open a small boutique agency out of her home, with Clairol as her first client. Knowing Linda was first and foremost a creative copywriter, Sadove suggested she meet with Robin, who was an executive vice president and group account director at a rival agency. Robin, as it turns out, had been looking to move to another agency.

Over a shared bran muffin, Robin and Linda agreed to join forces.

And so the Kaplan Thaler Group was born with six employees on the seven-hundred-square-foot third floor of the brownstone where Linda and her family lived on Nineteenth Street in the Chelsea section of Manhattan, with Clairol's Herbal Essences as our first account. (Remember the ad with a woman having an orgasmic experience washing her hair? *Yes! Yes! Yes!* That's the one.)

None of us had run a business before. The furniture was

rented. We had no high-speed copier; we borrowed Clairol's on our way into meetings. But the one thing we did have in huge quantities was grit. We worked tirelessly 24/7, with more determination and passion than perhaps we even realized we could muster. And it paid off. We quickly won more business from Clairol, and within that first year, the Kaplan Thaler Group went from having one client to $80 million in billings, including clients such as the Red Cross and Toys "R" Us. The staff bulged to twenty-four. Every single one of us had to haul out one bag of trash at the end of the night because there wasn't enough money to hire a commercial garbage service. There were not enough chairs for everyone, creating an unusual incentive for people to get in early. In nice weather, staff would work on the roof. Often, presentations would be assembled on the floor.

"We were breaking every occupancy law in the books," Linda says, laughing.

Before long, the Kaplan Thaler Group became one of the fastest-growing agencies in the country. In 2012, the Kaplan Thaler Group merged with Publicis New York to become Publicis Kaplan Thaler, and the agency has more than $3 billion in billings and more than eight hundred employees.

YES, WE WORKED hard. Yes, we had grit. Yes, we are grateful for the fact that we had loving support—and not much else for a long time—to fall back on at home. And while our parents were not immigrants, our experience is not dissimilar from that of many first-generation Americans, fueled by hope and the need to succeed. There was no other option. And like many of our peers who have "made it," we have children who are more financially comfortable than we were. And it concerns us.

Put Your Hands in Your Pockets

It's hard not to want to protect your children from disappointment, rejection, and failure. But without it, they'd never get very far, as Linda learned firsthand:

"When our daughter, Emily, turned five, we bought her a pretty pink bicycle; we couldn't wait to teach her how to ride it. Week after week, we would patiently hold the tiny seat while Emily attempted to gain her balance, gently pushing her along so she could stay on the bike. But every time we let go, Emily would fall.

"Over the next two years, my husband and I took turns teaching Emily how to ride, each time repeating the same procedure, and each time watching her fall. We came to the sad realization that our darling daughter might one day win the presidency, but she was never going to win the Tour de France.

"On Emily's seventh birthday, as I was making one last valiant attempt to teach her, a bemused bike rider in his mid-seventies stopped and offered to help.

" 'I just don't think she's ever going to get the hang of it,' I said with a lump in my throat, and a kink in my lumbar.

" 'Anyone can learn to ride a bike. Let me show you.'

"The man walked over to Emily and had her sit down, place her hands on the handlebars, and put her feet on the pedals.

" 'Now, Mom, what you need to do,' he said confidently, 'is take your hands, and ever so carefully, put them in your pockets.'

" 'But, but . . .' I pleaded.

"The man gave Emily a gentle push. She fell. I rushed to pick her up, but he stopped me.

"Emily got up on the bike again, and fell again. My hands were trembling, but I kept them pinned to my pockets.

"Emily got up on the bike a third time, and kept on riding. And riding. She went on to became a proficient cyclist, and now, in her twenties, is an expert horseback rider, figure skater, and all-around wonderfully balanced young woman. I am proud to say I have had a hand in her many accomplishments. Mostly because I've had the good sense to keep both of them in my pockets."

The Four Ingredients of Grit

Failure is how we learn—it's how we develop and acquire grit. From our own experiences, and those of the countless successful people we have worked with across a wide array of industries, from writers and CEOs to lawyers and Broadway performers, we can say it is grit that got them, and us, where we are. Our research and experience tell us that grit can be broken down into four essential components:

Guts—Grit begins with the courage to take on a tough challenge, and not falter in the face of adversity. General George S. Patton famously defined courage as "fear holding on a minute longer." Guts is what gives you the confidence to take a calculated risk, to be daring (without being reckless). Guts is about putting yourself out there, declaring your intention to triumph, even if victory appears to be nowhere in sight.

Resilience—Some of the world's most notable high achievers have flunked or dropped out of school, been fired from their jobs, evicted from their homes, or dealt some other major setback that forced them to hit bottom. But they bounced back. Jerry Seinfeld got booed off the stage during his first stand-up gig. It took three attempts before Steven Spielberg was accepted by a film school. But neither let humiliation or failure diminish their conviction. Studies show that people with a high degree of grit are able to stay focused and motivated, whatever failures, obstacles, and adversities get in their way. George Foreman was a retired, overweight former two-time heavyweight champion when the threat of bankruptcy drove him to take up boxing gloves again at age forty-five. But he triumphed and reclaimed his heavyweight title, using his winnings to pay off his debt and launch George Foreman Grills. Today he's worth an estimated $200 million. Resilience is what gives grit its elasticity. It's what makes you follow opportunity to the ends of the earth—even if it reroutes you to North Dakota after you bought a ticket for Maui.

Initiative—By definition, initiative—being a self-starter—is what makes grit dynamic, what sets it in motion. Leaders are often judged by their ability to take the initiative. But some of the most compelling examples of initiative are found far from the boardroom or the battlefield. One of our favorites took place on the African savanna, where thirteen-year-old Richard Turere was devastated to discover that lions had killed his family's bull. What could prevent such an attack in the future? When the Masai boy patrolled the cattle pasture at night in an effort to keep the herd safe, he noticed that the prowling lions were scared off by the bouncing beam of his flashlight as he walked. Tinkering with scavenged solar-charging cells and flashlight parts, he created a "lions light" fence that effectively keeps the predators away. The moral of this story? You don't have to outweigh or outrun an opponent if you can outsmart them first.

Tenacity—Tenacity is the relentless ability to stay focused on a goal. This is perhaps the most recognizable trait associated with grit. We see it in every athlete who overcomes a setback or a loss to win an Olympic medal or a championship ring; in every Nobel winner who has sweated through thousands of failed experiments and dead ends before making some groundbreaking discovery that has changed her field; in every entrepreneur who spends years fighting to launch a new service or product that ends up changing the way we live. Tenacity requires industriousness and determination, a value that, in the wake of the Great Depression, brought America to its industrial peak in the twentieth century. But it is a quality that seems in shorter supply in today's digital age. Studies by people such as K. Anders Ericsson at Florida State University have shown it takes a minimum of ten years—and the right kind of focused attention—to master a skill at the highest levels and realize one's full potential. World-renowned cellist Pablo Casals, asked at the age of ninety-three why he continued to practice three hours a day, replied, "I'm beginning to notice some improvement."

The science of success is only beginning to be explored. And there is much to learn. But the great thing about grit is that working harder, smarter, more passionately, and longer is something we control, unlike the community we grew up in, the high school we attended, the money and resources our parents have, company politics, or the current state of the economy. It is *attainable* by each and every one of us. Even if we're not the smartest or most talented person in the room.

Right now there are millions of people who have the potential to become world-class musicians, bestselling authors, or professional athletes if they are able to draw upon the guts, resilience, initiative, and tenacity necessary to realize their potential. Could you be one of them? We invite you to take our Grit Quiz at www.grittogreat.com to help you find out how well you score on the four grit components and your areas for improvement. In the chapters ahead you'll find many helpful strategies on how to develop your grit to its full potential.

GRIT BUILDERS

Give some grit. As parents, mentors, friends, or bosses, we can encourage the development of grit in others by not only providing support and guidance but also allowing those around us to learn on their own. Positive feedback is important, but don't redo a direct report's lousy memo. Instead, tell them (nicely) how they can make it better. And the next time your kid asks for their favorite peanut butter and banana sandwich or macaroni and cheese, don't make it for them. Show them how to do it themselves. Who knows, you could be inspiring a lifelong love of cooking.

Do your to-do list. As a first grit exercise, make a list of those projects you want to get done, and commit to finishing at least one this week. It can be a small, mindless project such as cleaning out a drawer. Others may require more thought, such as reading up on a new subject that could be useful in your career or personal life. Commit yourself for one month to finish every project on that list. Knowing that you cannot give up will force you to overcome challenges and learn new things, proving to yourself that your abilities are not fixed—they can be developed.

Chapter 2

The Talent Myth

*Talent is cheaper than table salt. What separates the talented
individual from the successful one is a lot of hard work.*

—Stephen King

The next time you catch one of our Aflac commercials on television (we confess, the Aflac Duck was one of our agency's creations), we hope the thirty-second spot that flashes before your eyes may seem funny and effortless. You may even be wowed by its creativity. When we watch it, however, we see something very different, because we know how much sweat equity we, along with our dedicated Aflac clients, have invested in that brief ad. That single vignette starring our iconic white duck and some hapless humans took a year to make, with some thirty people assigned full-time to the project. It's true, our folks are an extremely talented flock—that duck has had a longer run than most Broadway hits.

But talent plays only a small part in the commercial's success. If we were to be honest, two other, far less celebrated qualities—stamina and resilience—are the real stars. Every person assigned to Team Duck has to prove that they have the mettle to make it through endless rounds of rejection, rewrites, budget cuts, bad test scores, and the countless other obstacles and dead ends that come between the start of the project and the "huzzah!" moment with the duck's half-minute turn on *Dancing with the Stars*. To viewers, of course, such advertising is all flash and dazzle, like a Roman candle that burns spectacularly for a moment but is gone before you can grab your friend or partner and kids to say, "You've gotta see this!" But the truth is that achievement in any field takes a huge amount of effort and hard work (not to mention a lot of caffeine and a truckload of doughnuts and pizza). Our point? Talent alone is overrated. In fact, we would argue it's worthless unless you apply it consistently, in the right ways. Without putting in the required hard work and sweat equity, talent is nothing more than a great masterpiece unpainted, a sonata unwritten, a scientific breakthrough undiscovered, an invention unrealized.

Psychological studies of gifted children have debunked the myth that talent alone leads to success, or that only a fraction of us are capable of rising to the top. Innate intelligence or remarkable talent alone isn't enough.

What's Your Grit Grade?

Psychologist Angela Duckworth, winner of the prestigious MacArthur Fellowship—known as the "Genius Grant"— runs a lab at the University of Pennsylvania to study this very issue. She had been a seventh-grade math teacher when she noticed that the smartest students didn't always do their best work, and weren't always at the top of the class. So she went back to graduate school to study what actually determines success. Convinced that hard work and application were crucial to success, she developed a simple twelve-point scale to measure grit, which she defined as a combination of passion and perseverance, to achieve long-term goals. In her research, her test proved to be highly accurate in predicting which students would rise to the top. At the US Military Academy, Duckworth's simple test predicted more accurately than the military's own rigorous vetting process which freshman cadets would survive the elite academy's grueling summer training program. Grit also proved to be the deciding trait among children who made it to the winner's circle at the National Spelling Bee. In the corporate world, Duckworth and her team used their grit scale to pinpoint which salespeople would earn the most money, and which would lose their jobs.

"In all those very different contexts, one characteristic emerged as a significant predictor of success," Duckworth found. "And it wasn't social intelligence. It wasn't good looks, physical health, and it wasn't IQ. It was grit." In fact, her research revealed that, in certain instances, there was actually a negative correlation between high IQ and grit. Those with high IQ were used to working less to achieve a goal, and so, when they were confronted with very difficult tasks, they often gave up more quickly than those with lower scores. Perhaps because the people with comparatively lower IQs, in order to compensate, had developed a "grittier" attitude toward problem solving.

Duckworth also found that those with grit are in it for the long haul, not only able to finish a given task but also driven to relentlessly pursue it over several years. "The gritty individual approaches achievement as a marathon," Duckworth says in her research. People with grit are also less prone to frequently switch careers, opting instead to be laser-beam focused on achieving a single goal. Nor do they rely on positive feedback to spur them on and keep them motivated. As a result, the gritty individual will often pursue goals that are extremely challenging, and ones that may not be recognized, or appreciated, for decades to come.

The Failure of Standardized Tests

Some of the most accomplished people in history—including Ben Franklin and Charles Dickens—never made it through grade school. Thomas Edison's mother homeschooled him after his teacher concluded that the boy, destined to become one of the world's most prolific and ingenious inventors, was addle-brained. Ringo Starr and Elton John rose to pop culture superstardom despite being considered mediocre students and dropping out of high school; the famed Beatles drummer, a sickly boy who spent three years of his childhood in the hospital, was reportedly barely literate when he left school at fifteen.

When Thomas J. Stanley, author of the mega-bestseller *The Millionaire Mind,* surveyed more than one thousand millionaires, he found that their average SAT score was just 1190, a little above average at that time but far below what is needed to gain admittance to Harvard, Stanford, or most of the other elite colleges and universities.

Even high-powered tech companies like Google have realized they need to reconsider what best predicts the potential value of a future employee.

"Google famously used to ask everyone for a transcript, and G.P.A.s and test scores, but we don't anymore, unless you're just a few years out of school. We found that they don't predict anything," Laszlo Bock, Google's senior vice president in charge of people operations, told the *New York Times* in an interview. "What's interesting," he went on, "is the proportion of people without any college education at Google has increased over time as well." College graduates, especially those fresh out of school, are conditioned to give the specific answers they know their professors want, Bock hypothesized. But Google wants people "figuring out stuff where there is no obvious answer."

What's happening at Google is reflective of an overall shift in what recruiters are looking for during the hiring process. Dean Stamoulis of Russell Reynolds Associates, an executive leadership and search firm specializing in C-level and board member recruiting, says, "The emphasis in senior executive recruiting used to be on intelligence. Today, however, I believe the next frontier is assessing candidates for 'results intelligence'—a certain kind of 'smarts' that help an individual find results across a variety of situations." To Stamoulis, results intelligence is very similar to grit. It's the demonstrated ability to deliver under pressure, "to get beat up and bounce back when faced with difficulty and not be a whiner. The most effective leaders are those who never see themselves as victims of other people's actions, they don't blame and they don't rationalize. They often have an intrepid instinct."

While it may have taken recruiters years to catch up to the shift in thinking, scientists have been looking for some time now at whether basic intelligence can predict success. One of the most fascinating studies on the nature of talent was led by psychologist Lewis Terman, one of the founders of the standard IQ test. Terman was convinced that child prodigies were destined to lead the country, and in the 1920s, he set about identifying them. Terman's project would end up tracking 1,500 children identified as geniuses based on IQ tests over the course of their entire lifetimes. His subjects were nicknamed the "Termites." The Termites were superachievers by most traditional measures of success. Most graduated from college several years ahead of their nongifted peers, and landed professional jobs in greater numbers, which meant, of course, that they earned bigger salaries. But not all of the child geniuses were success stories. Some couldn't hold jobs at all. Others struggled with substance abuse. Twenty-two committed suicide.

And not a single one achieved the fame or made the outsize contributions to society that Lewis Terman had predicted. Innate intelligence or talent may have afforded them an early advantage in life and career, but no guarantees. As it turned out, two of the students Terman had passed over for his study—they didn't quite measure up—went on to win Nobel Prizes. Not a single Termite did.

In fact, sometimes the least likely people exceed everyone's expectations. Melissa was eight months pregnant when she gave birth to her third child. Her doctor told her that because of complications from the delivery, her daughter was oxygen deprived for a few precious moments, and there was a possibility she would have a developmental disability. Melissa decided to not share this news with anyone except her husband. And over time, she instilled in her daughter Ariel a strong work ethic, praising her not so much for her grades, which were often below average, but for her tenacity and perseverance.

Ariel ended up attending a fourth-tier college but became passionately interested in sociology, earned a master's degree in the subject, and is now pursuing a successful career in that field.

No one ever told Ariel her IQ was below normal, and perhaps because of that, she was allowed to realize her unlimited potential by exercising her dogged determination to work harder than her peers.

So why do scientists now believe that grit is a more relevant and reliable predictor of accomplishment in life? Because it speaks to one's character. Unlike talent, character is shaped by our experiences, by exposure to other people and to the situations we encounter in life—and our response to them. Character is something you can mindfully develop over time, regardless of income, education, or connections. It is the reason an unwanted child raised in poverty, with shoes that never fit and adults who never cared, grew into an inspirational role model for countless businesspeople and entrepreneurs.

Never Cut Corners

Before reading his autobiography, we never would have guessed that Dave Thomas, founder of the famed Wendy's restaurant chain, had suffered such a challenging and miserable upbringing. Born to an unwed New Jersey couple during the Depression, Dave was put up for adoption when he was six months old. His adoptive mother died of rheumatic fever when Dave was just five, leaving him to be raised by an unloving father and a series of stepmothers. Dave learned early on to make do with what he had; his feet were permanently deformed from years of wearing shoes he had long since outgrown. The family moved constantly, as Dave's father, a laborer, searched for work. At twelve, Dave lied about his age and got his first job delivering groceries, only to be fired over a misunderstanding with his boss about vacation. Dave spent the summers in Michigan with his

maternal grandmother, who gave him the only sense of security he ever knew growing up. He would quote Grandma
Minnie's sage advice decades later, after he had become a
grandfather himself: "Hard work is good for the soul," she
would say. "And it keeps you from feeling sorry for yourself,
because you don't have time."

When he became a counter boy in a mom-and-pop
diner, Dave found a sense of connection and family in the
restaurant business that he'd never felt at home. He hap-
pily worked twelve-hour shifts before the age of thirteen,
letting his schoolwork fall by the wayside. Even doing scut
work in the kitchen, he felt like a vital part of something—
that he belonged. When his father packed up to move again,
Dave refused to go, renting a room at the YMCA and dropping out of school to support himself. He was barely fifteen
years old. By the time he was thirty, Dave was bristling with
ideas of establishing his own restaurant; he jumped at the
chance to buy four failing chicken carryouts in Columbus,
Ohio, off the hands of an old-timer named Colonel Harland
Sanders. Dave turned the franchises around and sold them
back to Kentucky Fried Chicken for more than $1.5 mil-
lion. Even though he was only in his thirties at the time,
Dave could have retired, but didn't. Instead, he used that
money to finance his own dream: launching a chain of fast-
food restaurants that would operate on another principle
Grandma Minnie had instilled in him. "Don't cut corners,
or you'll lose quality." She used to tell him, no matter what
task Dave was undertaking, "If you lose quality, you lose
everything else." Thomas named his restaurant Wendy's,

after his youngest daughter, and applied Grandma Minnie's advice liberally and literally to the hamburgers he served. Every patty was perfectly square, no corners cut.

Wendy Thomas told us how she used to ride along with her dad while he made the rounds visiting the franchises in the restaurant chain he owned and named after her. Wendy still lights up at the memory of her father meeting Wendy's employees, greeting customers, hanging out in his favorite spot—behind the grill—and talking about ways to make what was already a great business even better. Complacency wasn't a word in his vocabulary. He had zero tolerance for it in the people he entrusted to help run his empire, which he ultimately created for his children—not to ensure that they never had to work, but to ensure that they would know how to. He wanted to give them something more valuable than trust funds and a life of leisure: He wanted Wendy and her siblings to develop the same grit and work ethic that his own hardscrabble childhood had instilled in him.

Dave Thomas's kids were expected to earn their own way in the world. "Do what you want to do," Wendy remembers her dad urging her as she went off to college. "Just make sure you really like it. If you want to dig ditches, dig ditches, but do it with pride. You've got to have integrity in everything you do." Many people think of work in terms of what it takes *out* of you; Wendy was taught early on what work instilled *in* you.

Sadly, the world lost Dave in 2003. The impact of his death was felt throughout the Wendy's organization, and among the American public, which had gotten to "know" him as the star in more than eight hundred Wendy's commercials over thirteen years. His plainspoken affability made him an American folk hero. After his passing, Wendy's struggled through a series of advertising campaigns and agencies trying to reignite the spirit of Dave, without much success.

The Recipe for Success

In the summer of 2009, we heard that the fast-food chain was looking for a new advertising agency. Wendy's had spent more than $275 million in media advertising the previous year. All of Madison Avenue was salivating over the prospect of winning the Wendy's account.

We thought we were the perfect agency to help them. But seventy-five other agencies felt the same way. To win the account, we knew we would have to put together a creative campaign that would leave our competitors in the dust. Winning the Wendy's account would be a game changer for our agency. It would be the single largest piece of business we had brought in so far. Since founding the Kaplan Thaler Group in a cramped brownstone twelve years earlier, we had grown dramatically—and acquired high-rise offices in the most expensive part of town. But even with major clients like Aflac, Pfizer, and Procter & Gamble, we were still the underdogs in this particular battle. We work in a male-dominated industry full of agencies that had been around so long they probably carved media campaigns into cave walls

("Mastodon, the new white meat"), and our agency was still a small and scrappy newcomer.

"We're perfect for this account," Linda blurted out to our staff at an early brainstorming session. "You know why? We share the same business DNA that Dave Thomas had. The other guys can outstaff us and outspend us, but they cannot outwork us." We ordered copies of *Dave's Way,* the autobiography Dave Thomas had published in the nineties, for everyone working on the account, and memorized it cover to cover. We were all inspired by his humble wisdom. And the more we thought about the grit Dave showed, the more parallels we saw between his philosophy and ours. But philosophy is easy; putting together a killer two-hour presentation in less than two months was going to be hard. Really hard. Like Dave, we faced each day as underdogs, putting in the kind of sweat equity that would prove we were grittier than our competition.

We faced each workday with the stubborn determination that we would become number one. We went into battle for the Wendy's account with the mantra "What would Dave do?" and made a conscious effort to match his drive and conviction every step of the way. Job one? Hit the road, as Dave used to do, and visit as many Wendy's franchises as we could. We wanted to talk to the people who ran the restaurants and to the customers who ate there. Like Dave, we wanted to get behind the grill.

Robin and our team donned aprons and worked in restaurants across the country chopping salad, making chili, and learning firsthand what Wendy's refers to as "the build of each hamburger." We gained enormous on-the-ground information about Wendy's, a few culinary skills, and an affinity for the unparalleled pleasures of a hot, crispy Wendy's fry dunked in a Classic Chocolate Frosty (okay, there were some perks to the job).

Back in New York, we worked seventy-hour weeks on our pitch. Every conference room at the agency smelled of french fries and hamburgers; we ordered Wendy's every day and ate our way through the entire menu. We researched where each ingredient came from, including the farms where the lettuce and tomatoes were harvested. We began videotaping our meetings to make sure we captured every insight, every scrap of conversation, never knowing when the germ of an idea might emerge. We spent our Fourth of July weekend hanging out with focus groups and guests at Wendy's restaurants. Every day, we held a mandatory Wendy's war room session with all our creative, media, PR, in-store, research, and account teams. We scrutinized the work everyone had done and brutally critiqued it. Ideas surfaced and then were swatted away like flies in a never-ending search for the insight that would spark what we call a Bang idea—a game changer for Wendy's. Vacations were canceled, 8 p.m. meetings became routine. We even held a Wendy's "sleepover" for the teams.

We would like to tell you that all that hard work meant everything was locked and loaded well ahead of the due date. But the truth is, a week away from the final presentation, we had conference rooms full of our work but nothing we felt was a winner. Undaunted, we spent the next four sleep-less nights in a creative frenzy, putting together 25 TV ads, 40 radio spots, 70 billboards, bus signs, print ads, and the like, as well as a complete redesign of Wendy's in-store signs and other materials. We redesigned their website, created an original song to underscore it all, and topped it off with a parting souvenir for all the Wendy's executives (a mock *USA Today* front page with the headline "Wendy's Surpasses Burger King with the Help of New Agency"). We intended to put on the equivalent of a Broadway show for Wendy's. There was only one small problem: most Broadway shows rehearse for months, and our clock had just run out.

We had one night to choreograph the entire presen-tation.

With the big day in front of us, we packed ten huge black bags with presentation boards to take with us to the confer-ence center hotel in Columbus, Ohio. We still had an over-whelming amount of work to do before our presentation the following morning. So we split into two teams: Robin took the media, strategy, and account people; Linda took the creative people. When Robin came by at midnight to say hello, she discovered Linda and the creative team punch-drunk with exhaustion. Peanut shells covered the suite floor. Yet so far they had only two spots rehearsed. *What on earth was taking so long?* Robin wondered. Even though we felt confident that the work was great, we knew that selling an idea has as much to do with the way you present it as it does with the idea itself. Every sound level had to be checked. We needed to figure out the choreography—who would stand where. Scripts needed to be memorized so the presenter could make eye contact with the client. Jokes that were falling flat needed to be rewritten. It was clearly going to be an all-nighter, and even then it seemed doubtful that Linda's team would be able to pull it all together in time for the morning presentation. But nobody was ready to say "We tried our best" and give in to fatigue. The unspoken rallying cry that got us through that long, stressful night was *We can do this!*

By the time we entered the room the next morning, we had two hours until showtime. The temptation to just try to relax and find a Zen-like calm was strong. But we knew we had to muster our last ounce of grit in the final hour. "We have just enough time for one dress rehearsal!" we cried, rallying the troops yet again. When it was our turn to face Wendy's judges, we were as ready as we could possibly be.

And the presentation, we were convinced afterward, was flawless.

The next day, Wendy's sent an actress dressed as the company's bubbly, freckle-faced mascot—complete with bright red pigtails—to deliver the news. We summoned the entire agency, since virtually everyone had worked on the pitch, to read the congratulatory letter from Wendy's, telling us we had won their business, passing it from hand to hand so everyone could have a look.

When we asked Wendy's why they chose us, they told us that they loved our work (although they had seen some stellar ideas from the other agencies, too) but above all came away convinced that no one would work harder on their business than we would. And we proved them right, as a few years later, Wendy's did surpass Burger King as the number-two hamburger chain in America.

TALENT MAY HAVE gotten us noticed, but grit got us the booking. Mark Murphy, founder and CEO of Leadership IQ, a consulting company that does research and leadership training for organizations like IBM, Microsoft, General Electric, and Johns Hopkins University, agrees. For his book *Hiring for Attitude,* Murphy spent three years studying twenty thousand new hires. He found that 46 percent of them failed within eighteen months. "The shocker," he reports, is that "only 11 percent of those failed for lack of technical skills."

The rest didn't make it because of their attitude: poor motivation, negativity, and emotional issues made them lackluster team players, ineffective leaders, inconsistent problem solvers, and, worst of all, a drain on their workplace's collective energy. Most probably had the smarts for the job—what they lacked was the optimism, grit, and determination to succeed.

Bottom line: you don't need to be a Mensa member to be a success in today's competitive work world, whether you're pursuing an entry-level job, a managerial position, a big promotion, or the venture capital to strike out on your own. You need grit.

GRIT BUILDERS

Become an overpreparer. Talent is a good thing, but don't let overconfidence get in the way of success. Practice. Do a dress rehearsal. If you have a talk to present at school or work, say it out loud in front of a mirror, or video yourself on your phone. Think of all the angles. Working just a little harder than someone else who might be just as talented (or even a bit more) is what will win the day.

First get the gig. We're not telling people to lie, but rather to push yourself. When asked to take on an unfamiliar task that you may not feel qualified for, look for an aspect of the opportunity that resonates with your previous experience, or with your interest in learning something new. Think of how your strengths might be an asset, rather than automatically questioning whether you can do the job before you have it. And remember, if they asked you to do it, they already believe you can.

Go the extra thirty minutes. You'd be surprised at the edge you can develop by applying yourself for an extra half hour on something—a goal, a skill, a job. Pick the time of day when you are most productive (early morning, after a jog, or in the quiet of a Sunday evening) and instead of watching a sitcom, devote yourself to whatever "it" might be. A half hour each day adds up to 180 hours of extra practice a year!

CHAPTER 3

Ditch the Dream

I never dreamed about success. I worked for it.

—ESTÉE LAUDER

IN OUR DREAMS, WE ALWAYS GET TO BE THE DIRECTOR, star, scriptwriter, stage manager, costume designer, lighting technician, and, of course, appreciative audience. We do our own stunts, write our own reviews, and sweep our award shows. If the plot doesn't hold our attention, our subconscious mind instantly conjures a new one. When the alarm clock sounds, it's no wonder most of us hit the snooze button—we want to linger in dreamland just a little longer. So much is going on there.

Except, of course, life.

There's an old Yiddish proverb that, loosely translated, goes something like this: *If you want your dreams to become reality, wake up already.*

Too often, the whole gauzy adage of "following your dream" has taken the place of more attainable aspirations: setting your sights on a goal, formulating a plan, charting a path, steadily working your way forward from milepost to milepost. While the dreamers are still sleeping, the doers are taking victory laps, because they had the sense to wake up and get to work. They put themselves in a grit state of mind.

Along Came a Bestseller

Linda saw resounding proof of this when she befriended a colleague at the J. Walter Thompson ad agency back when she was a junior copywriter. Jim became the chief creative officer and CEO, and Linda ended up working for him as a creative director for more than fifteen years. Even with his demanding executive job, Jim would get up before dawn every day so he could work on his novel for four hours before coming to work. The books he quietly churned out over the years found publishers and a small, appreciative audience, but no real success. Jim still kept rolling out of bed in the dead of night to keep at it. Whenever he had downtime during the day, he would whip out a legal pad and start scribbling away. That's what he was doing one day on a business trip to Rochester, New York, to work on the Kodak account. He was blithely oblivious to Linda sitting beside him on the plane, terrified, digging her nails into his arm and shrieking at intervals; anyone less good-humored would have found this annoying (her fear of flying cannot be exaggerated).

"At some point, Jim looks up from his pad and his eyes

light up and he says, 'I figured it out!'" Linda remembers. His excitement was enough to distract her from the mental movie in her mind of their plane bursting into flames and nosediving to earth.

"Figured out what?" she asked. Did he know something about their impending death that she hadn't realized?

"How to write a bestseller!" Jim replied.

Linda glanced skeptically at the yellow legal pad filled with his longhand.

"How?" she wondered.

"I've always believed in compelling characters, but given the pace of life these days, most people would probably prefer to read short chapters. With a cool twist at the end of every single one," Jim said triumphantly.

Which is exactly how he wrote—in longhand—*Along Came a Spider,* the first of one hundred and ten *New York Times* bestsellers he has had to date, a record that has helped make James Patterson the top-selling writer of all time, with some three hundred and five million readers worldwide.

We love telling the story of James Patterson's success partly because he is the embodiment of grit when it comes to tenacity and initiative—but also because he's a poster child for the difference between having a dream and having a goal. He didn't spend all day at the ad agency earning his paycheck, while merely fantasizing about becoming a famous novelist. He picked up a pen and wrote. Every unpublished word he scrawled on his legal pad led him closer to the bestseller list. He had a dream, but more important, he set it in motion. Action turned it into reality.

"What If" Gets You Nowhere

It's easy to live in the sweet fantasyland of if, if, if. Everyone enjoys fantasizing about the future, and furnishing their Powerball castles in the air. But too often we wrap ourselves in the same cozy blanket of possibility whether we're thinking about winning the lottery, or winning a promotion at work—and it is a mistake that can cost you dearly. Recent research suggests that there's a serious flaw in the "dream it into happening" approach to achieving our goals. Visualization can actually be more detrimental than useful when it comes to realizing goals. That's because, unlike elite athletes, who first popularized visualization training, we tend to fast-forward the fantasy to the good part, picturing ourselves accepting the gold medal, rather than visualizing us training for it, and anticipating injuries or other obstacles and setbacks along the way. Researchers found that the fantasy gives us a feel-good buzz, which robs us of the motivation to get off our butts and do the work to achieve the real thing. It creates expectations of instant success. And when reality turns out to be harder than we imagined, our performance falls short, our motivation evaporates, and our anxiety increases. We're actually in a worse state than we would have been if we had just ditched the dream in the first place and replaced it with a strong measure of grit and self-initiative. Daydreams are a quick-hit cheap thrill. Replaying them again and again while wondering why they don't come true is like watching *Chariots of Fire* and experiencing the feel-good endorphins the movie creates in you, and then wondering why you don't have a runner's conditioning when the movie's over.

In her study of fantasy versus expectation, New York University psychology professor Gabriele Oettingen found that freshly minted graduates who spent more time dreaming about their ideal job fared worse than peers who refused to indulge in such fantasies. The dreamers, two years later, had applied for fewer jobs, received fewer offers, and, once employed, had lower salaries. Why? Thinking about an idealized future can feign having already attained the dream, and detract from the effort of reaching success. Despite what the self-help and coaching industry wants us to believe, positive thinking should not be about the outcome of your dreams, but about all the roadblocks in the way and what you can do to move past them.

Raise Your Own Baton

With grit, even impossible dreams can be realized. Marin Alsop discovered hers at the age of nine, when she was learning to play the violin. Her father took her to see Leonard Bernstein conduct the New York Philharmonic in a Young People's Concert. But it wasn't the violin section young Marin was fixated on: it was the conductor himself. "That's what I want to be!" she announced to her father. Her violin teacher quickly doused her passion, telling Marin that girls did not become conductors. And it was true—there were no women conductors blazing a path Marin might follow. The harsh reality of her teacher's dismissal devastated Marin, and infuriated her mother. "You can be whatever you want to be," Ruth Alsop told her daughter. The next morning, when Marin came downstairs for breakfast, a long wooden box was waiting for her on the table. It was full of batons.

Alsop pursued her violin studies, eventually getting her master's in performance from the Juilliard School. Her real dream was to be a conductor—but the world's major orchestras were still all conducted by men. Although her goal appeared to be out of reach, Alsop never let it out of sight. She spent hours in front of the mirror with the stereo on, conducting invisible orchestras with her baton. She bribed Juilliard classmates with pizza and beer to bring their instruments to her apartment so she could practice conducting. She made her living as a freelance violinist while she studied conducting under the esteemed Carl Bamberger. And when she still couldn't get a break or the practical experience she needed, she took what seemed to her like the next perfectly logical step: she formed her own orchestra.

Finally, after winning the coveted Leonard Bernstein Conducting Fellowship at the Tanglewood Music Center one summer and becoming a protégé of Bernstein himself, Alsop made some headway, debuting with the Philadelphia Orchestra and the Los Angeles Philharmonic, before being named musical director of the Colorado Symphony. Granted, Colorado isn't considered a top-tier orchestra. But Alsop managed, through guest appearances and recordings, to become more well known, particularly as an ardent promoter of contemporary music. In 2005 she became the only conductor to ever receive the prestigious MacArthur Fellowship. But for all the accolades, she still hadn't achieved her dream.

Forty-two years passed between the moment Marin Alsop knew what she wanted to do with her life and the moment she realized her goal. In 2007, at the age of fifty-one, Alsop took the podium as the new musical director of the Baltimore Symphony Orchestra.

She was the first woman in the world to lead a major orchestra.

So how do you separate dreams from goals, fantasy from reality? It means taking stock of what you want to achieve and making that first bold move to make it happen. A move that, for Fabiano Caruana, would change the course of his life.

Seize the Initiative

In chess, seizing the initiative means a player has made a move that forces his opponent to respond to him, that puts his opponent on the defensive and allows the player to have an advantage on the board. Fabiano Caruana, who began playing chess when he was five years old, realized very early on that he wanted to take whatever initiative necessary to become a world champion—a rather lofty and audacious goal for a first grader. But, unlike other kids, who might just daydream about their ambitions, Fabiano began studying for hours each day, competing in hundreds of tournaments, and taking several chess lessons a week. Fortunately, Fabiano's parents supported their son's aspirations, but they also knew it would take years of dedication, focus, and sacrifice for him to achieve his goal.

When Fabiano was twelve, the family decided that he would be homeschooled, allowing him more time to study chess. They moved from New York to Spain, giving their son the opportunity to study with Russian international master Boris Zlotnik. Over the next several years, Fabiano and his family moved from Hungary to Switzerland and back again to Spain so that Fabiano could benefit from the tutelage of the world's best chess trainers.

Fabiano's tenacity and perseverance have paid off. At age twenty-three, Fabiano Caruana is a chess grand master, with a chess rating of 2819, making him the number-two-ranked player in the world. And many in the chess community believe that one day soon he will become number one.

When we asked Fabiano's dad why they decided to uproot their lives so that their son could pursue his passion for chess, he told us, "My wife and I believe that all of us are far more capable than we realize, but that to fully develop that capability we need to be willing to exert the hard work necessary for success. Our son had a dream, and our job was to do everything humanly possible to help him make it come true."

Fabiano had a single-minded goal, one that was unwavering from the time he was in grade school. For many of us, our goals are not always that fixed. Over time, we may decide to set our sights in a totally different direction. But to do that, we need to reroute our path to success.

Move the Goalposts

Neither of us had advertising on our dream list when we set out in life. Robin had always been told she was good at drawing. By the time she reached college, she "kind of got trapped into being an art major." Being competent at something doesn't necessarily make it fulfilling, though, and Robin soon realized that while she was good at drawing, she wasn't great, and furthermore, she didn't really like it all that much. When she boiled down the artist dream to see what she could extract from it, she discovered that what she loved was creating the ideas, not the actual execution. She was a creative thinker, not a maker. She reset her sights and enrolled in an ad design program at Syracuse University.

Linda started out with a different dream, as well. The stage had always beckoned her. She enjoyed acting, stand-up comedy, and songwriting. But after she received a callback for the off-Broadway show *National Lampoon's Lemmings* and found out the part she auditioned for had gone to the enormously funny Gilda Radner, Linda had a life-changing revelation. She realized that she had some talent as a comedic actress, but did not have the stamina to endure endless auditions and rejections to get her where she wanted to be. She decided then and there to stop fixating on an imaginary future in a world in which she could never excel. Moreover, she discovered that passion isn't sustained by a fantasy or a dream—it needs a destination and guidance. Advertising gave Linda a place to be funny, creative, and in charge. And the paychecks were better, too. While she had performed some original songs in her early twenties, it wasn't until she heard a kid singing the Toys "R" Us jingle she had written ("I don't want to grow up, I'm a Toys 'R' Us kid") on his way to the bus that she knew she had finally achieved her dream.

Of course, goals must be regularly reevaluated. Do the goals you had at twenty still fit when you're thirty? Or forty? A recent Harris poll found that only 14 percent of US workers believe they have the perfect job; more than half want to change careers altogether. Younger people have adapted to the changing marketplace by becoming adept at perpetual motion. The Pew Research Center found that millennials— those born between 1980 and the early 2000s—averaged seven job changes during their twenties, and that six out of ten changed careers at least once. Remember, aspirations are not one-size-fits-all, nor do they all have the same shelf life.

What we need to do is to prioritize our ambitions and goals, ranking them from easiest to achieve to hardest to achieve, and from most important to least important to our lives. If something is hard to achieve ("travel around the world by motorcycle") and not terribly important ("someday, just to say I did"), scratch it. If it's tough ("lose thirty pounds") and crucial ("prediabetic, daughter's wedding next summer") then get started by tackling it through one-a-day tasks: find local gyms with free one-day passes; visit each one; choose a gym; consult with a nutritionist/personal trainer to come up with workout routine and meal plan; shop for three days' worth of meals, etc. Before you know it, you're halfway to your goal, instead of frozen at the starting point. Taking that first step on a high wire is always scary but grit allows us to reach heights we never thought possible before. And when it comes to taking risks, the best way to achieve your goals is to never look down.

GRIT BUILDERS

Touch the totem. Sticking with a goal you have settled on can be tough. Remind yourself of what you are trying to achieve. Do what blogger Mauricio Estrella did and make your goal your password, such as quit@smoking4ever. After all, most of us type a password many times per day. This trick can remind yourself of what you are trying to achieve.

Conduct a reality check. Take note of how often you daydream about changing something in your life. Next, promise yourself you will spend the same amount of time creating an action plan to make that change happen. Your plan should include everything that needs to get done to attain the goal, plotted against a timeline. To write this book, we knew exactly how many words we needed to write each day in order to meet our deadline. We used the word count feature so we could see our constant progress toward the end of each chapter. Keep your list visible, or add reminders to an electronic calendar. See how great it feels to check things off the list. A dream is only a mirage if it doesn't lead to an opportunity to make it a reality.

Listen up! If friends and family are always telling you what a terrific dancer you are, they may be on to something. Pay attention to what people say and see that you are good at. Build on it.

CHAPTER 4

Lose the Safety Net

A ship is always safe at the shore——but that is not what it is built for.

—ALBERT EINSTEIN

NIK WALLENDA WAS A LITTLE MORE THAN HALFWAY across the 1,400-foot tightrope he had rigged across the Grand Canyon when he felt his balance falter and the cable bounce. He crouched to sit a moment, hoping to steady both himself and the wire. The breathtaking stunt was being broadcast live (with a ten-second delay, for obvious reasons) by the Discovery Channel. With no harness or safety net, sheer grit was the only thing keeping Wallenda from plunging 1,500 feet to the canyon floor as the world watched. "It was just getting really, really uncomfortable," he told interviewers afterward. "I didn't know if I wanted to get up at all. I just wanted to sit there and call out for Mommy."

Wallenda's feat—one of his seven world records—made us think about the purpose of the safety nets we so routinely seek in our everyday lives. Are they coaxing us forward, offering us the protection we need, or holding us back? So we asked Wallenda, a thirty-seven-year-old father of three, for his take on safety nets, and he graciously shared with us the wisdom gleaned from a legendary seven-generation family of high-wire artists.

"Our minds are extremely powerful," he told us. "You can learn to control what comes in, and filter out the negative. Fear is negative. You can either be overtaken by it, or you can overcome it."

Performing without a safety net, to Wallenda, is more of an assertion that he is *in* control than a scary reminder of what could happen should he lose it. It's not that he has a false sense of security, or a cavalier attitude toward risk. But we found that what Wallenda does applies just as much to those of us who prefer to view the Grand Canyon by tour bus—a grit mindset that can help us conquer the comparatively mundane risks each of us face in our lives. It comes down to becoming, in essence, your own first responder: identifying worst-case scenarios ahead of time, then training yourself what to do if and when they occur. Should that moment arrive, you will have the training—and the confidence—to calmly respond, rather than hastily react. This is where guts, resilience, initiative, and tenacity truly pay off. All it takes is mindfulness—an ability to zoom in on the problem at hand.

"Some are born with grit, and it comes easier," Wallenda

allowed. But, he went on, "we are all growing, all the time. You can gain more and more of it, or you can also lose it if you don't practice it. Scary is not in my vocabulary. Fear is really just a deep respect. I clearly remember the first time I grasped this: I was six or seven years old and sitting on my father's shoulders while he was riding a bicycle across the wire. I had been around wild animals in the circus all my life—elephants, tigers, chimpanzees—but I was never afraid of them. I was raised to respect them, knowing they could kill me. On top of my father's shoulders that day, even though I knew it was something my dad could do in his sleep, I still felt this jolt. I understood that I could either sit there and shake and tremble, or tell myself to be calm and collected. I chose not to be scared. I realized that I'm in control of my mind—my mind is not in control of me."

Although performing on the high wire has long since become second nature to Wallenda, he continues to respect what could hurt him. That keen awareness and respect, in turn, has taught him to prepare for the worst so he can do his best. He and his team spent five years studying terrain and conditions in the Grand Canyon before undertaking the stunt described at the beginning of the chapter. While there was no way to predict how much fine desert dust might settle on his two-inch-wide cable the day of his walk, or how powerful the upward drafts of hot air from the canyon floor might get, Wallenda prepared himself for those conditions and rehearsed maneuvers he could do in response. Before the Grand Canyon walk, he practiced for hours every day in his Florida backyard, using wind machines to create 91-mph gusts—stronger than any ever recorded in the canyon itself. When Tropical Storm Andrea slammed ashore in Florida a week before Wallenda's historic walk, he seized the opportunity to experience the unpredictability of the fierce storm by practicing on a thirty-five-foot-high wire in the wind and rain. When the momentous day came and Wallenda found himself making his way across the gorge and feeling the wire bounce beneath his slippered feet, he reminded himself: *You trained for ninety-mile-per-hour winds, even though they never get above sixty here. You prepared for this; you know what to do.* As he neared the other side, Wallenda broke into a sprint, and nimbly leapt back onto solid ground, before going home to ponder what challenge to take on next.

When confidence becomes a muscle memory, panic is replaced by peak performance.

Go on Autopilot

Flight attendants are trained to evacuate a jumbo jet filled with passengers in ninety seconds or less (in the United States, it's a federal requirement). Airlines and training academies drill trainees over and over again using realistic mock cabins and simulated emergencies, such as a crash or fire.

Lee Yoon-Hye put her training to the test on July 6, 2013, when Asiana Flight 214 hit a seawall on approach to San Francisco International Airport, broke apart, then cartwheeled down the runway and burst into flames when the jet's fuel ignited. You might remember seeing news images of Lee: the petite forty-year-old cabin manager from Seoul, South Korea, could be spotted carrying passengers to safety on her back. What you didn't see was the phenomenal grit she displayed inside the Boeing 777 cabin, where an emergency slide had deployed within the wreckage, trapping terrified passengers. Lee grabbed an axe so that a copilot could puncture the slide. Seeing flames erupting in the back, she tossed a fire extinguisher to another crew member as she began herding passengers to safety. All but three of the 307 people aboard the plane survived. And not surprisingly, Lee was the last one off. The San Francisco fire chief hailed her as a hero; doctors later discovered Lee had been assisting the evacuation with a fractured tailbone.

"We followed our training," she modestly told reporters afterward. "I wasn't really thinking, but my body just started carrying out the steps needed for an evacuation."

The fear and trepidation most of us face in our daily lives falls far short of having to save trapped passengers in a burning plane or potentially free-falling to the bottom of the Grand Canyon. Yet we routinely rig our lives with the kinds of safety nets that would suggest otherwise. If you wait to act in a situation until it's risk-free before venturing a toe out onto your own proverbial high wire, what you're really risking is a lifetime frozen at the starting line. A woman creates a multimillion-dollar business she started online in her dorm room, while her ex-boyfriend shows up at the class reunion with a job he hates and vague proclamations about waiting to get all of his ducks in a row. Sound familiar? Perhaps you fantasize about taking salsa lessons but refuse to sign up until you lose twenty pounds because you want to look good. Or you're heartsick over your town's plans to level a small old-growth forest for a strip mall, but can't summon the time, energy, and political savvy to fight it. Rolling over is a lot less painful than falling on one's face.

Too often, our typical default setting is to fear disaster, rather than actually plan for it. And that, Nik Wallenda tells us, is the true catastrophe.

"It's easier to settle for what's comfortable than to push on and excel," he explains.

Too often, we live life avoiding what we fear, a hundred times a day. And what we fear often comes down to failure or rejection.

Get Rejected

When hypnotist Jason Comely invented an online game called Rejection Therapy a few years ago, one of his stated objectives was to teach people "to be more aware of how irrational social fears control and restrict our lives."

The game had only one rule: You *must* be rejected by someone every single day. In fact, rejection equaled success in the game. If your target didn't reject you, and instead granted your request, it counted as a failure because you evidently didn't ask for enough.

Chinese immigrant Jia Jiang came across the challenge after quitting his tech job in Austin, Texas, to devote six months to pursuing the dream he had hungered for ever since Bill Gates had spoken to his high school in Beijing: to become an entrepreneur. Four months into his six-month sabbatical, though, Jiang looked down at his vibrating phone in a restaurant to see a devastating text message from the major investor he thought he had on the hook to finance his start-up: *No,* was all it said. Jiang excused himself to go outside and cry.

"My choices were rejection or regret, and both stunk," Jiang recalled in a TEDx talk that has since made him a YouTube sensation. Jiang considered cutting his losses and going back to a "real" job two months early. "But in the end, I chose rejection and kept going, and the world was never the same again."

Intrigued by Comely's game, Jiang decided to desensitize himself to the pain of rejection by challenging himself to endure one hundred days of rejection, and record it on a hidden camera for his video blog. He immediately began racking up points. Costco refused to let him talk to its customers over the store intercom. A stranger declined to loan him a hundred bucks. FedEx wouldn't send a box to Santa at the North Pole. "But then a funny thing happened," Jiang reported. "I started getting yeses." He knocked on a stranger's door and was granted permission to play soccer in the family's backyard. A guard let him dance Gangnam-style on the building's security camera. Then there was the time Jiang walked into a random company and asked to speak to the CEO.

"Why?" the receptionist wanted to know.

"Because I'm going to challenge him to a staring contest," came the reply. And he was invited in to see the CEO. (The CEO turned out to be a *her,* and she won.)

Rejection, Jiang discovered, had turned him into "a better communicator, a better negotiator." And the customary sting he had experienced upon being rejected had been replaced by a feeling of liberation that he found exhilarating, pushing him to take ever-greater risks.

When Jiang strolled into a Krispy Kreme shop to request doughnuts customized to resemble the Olympics logo, an obliging employee said she'd see what she could do, then returned shortly to proudly display her creation—a box of five interlocked doughnut rings in the Olympic colors. "It's on me, get out," she said with a grin when Jiang asked what he owed. Jiang's hidden-camera video of that encounter drew so many viewers on YouTube that the media took note, and the rejected Jiang became a star.

His experiment, Jiang told his TED audience, "taught me to see rejection eye to eye and remain calm, and see it as what it is. It's not this monster bag of hurt that I thought. It's not some universal truth about who I am. It's just someone's opinion, and it says as much about that person as it does about me."

There's a big difference, Jiang pointed out, between remorse over not having done something, and rejection. Rejection is getting shot down and surviving; remorse is never taking flight in the first place.

He has yet to hear back on his hundredth request—an

interview with President Obama—but Jiang did score a yes he never foresaw the night he received the text message that had crushed his dreams: he landed a deal to publish a book about the power of rejection.

Facing constant rejection can be devastating. But it can also be the impetus you need to work harder than you ever thought possible.

Draw On Your Inner Resources

Selling a cartoon to *The New Yorker* magazine takes a Herculean amount of diligence, dedication, stamina, and grit. When Bob Mankoff first started out as a cartoonist, he submitted thousands of entries to *The New Yorker* before one was finally accepted for publication. Almost thirty years later, after penning some 950 *New Yorker* drawings, Mankoff is the cartoon editor of the magazine. He and his team laboriously sift through as many as two thousand entries a week, knowing that only seventeen or eighteen of them will make the cut. And many of the submissions are from regulars, talented artists who face an acceptance rate of only 10 percent. Yet they refuse to give up, drawing on a reservoir of creativity and wit that seems to be limitless. Mankoff believes their creativity is actually fueled by *The New Yorker*'s low acceptance rate; like a gambler's high, the artist never knows when, and which, of his drawings will be a winner. "Every so often," Mankoff told us, "you will get that jolt of positive reinforcement to fuel your resilience." It is often exactly the motivation artists need to reach deeper into their creative imagination and spur their sense of grit.

Go with Your Guts

The hypercompetitive tech industry, with its take-no-prisoners culture, seems to breed a lot of introspection about grit. As a female engineer in the testosterone-driven Silicon Valley, senior Google manager Sabrina Farmer frequently battled self-doubt and harsh self-criticism. She realized that questioning or downplaying her capabilities had become second nature. When an acquaintance mentioned plans to run a triathlon, Farmer instantly responded, "Oh, I could never do that!" Later, she found herself wondering: *Why not? What made me say that?* She summoned the grit to sign up for the race, train and compete, then went on to run a marathon. It wasn't, she confessed later, something she particularly enjoyed, but the insight it gave her was well worth the effort and agony. She realized that her habit of belittling herself served as an air cushion from failure's hard falls. But that emotional safety mechanism was also holding her back.

Farmer attributed her tentativeness to what psychologists call "impostor syndrome." In her book *The Secret Thoughts of Successful Women,* Valerie Young writes that people with impostor syndrome tend to dismiss their accomplishments and abilities "as merely a matter of luck, timing, outside help, charm—even computer error . . . that they've somehow managed to slip through the system undetected, in their mind it's just a matter of time before they're found out." And it strikes successful women more than any other group. It's what prompted actress Jodie Foster to confess on *60 Minutes* that she thought her Academy Award was "a fluke" and that "everybody would find out, and they'd take the Oscar back. They'd come to my house, knocking on the door, 'Excuse me, we meant to give that to someone else. That was going to Meryl Streep.'"

Now, when Sabrina finds herself clinging to the safety net of self-doubt, she stops to ask herself three questions:

What is the problem?

What's the worst that can happen?

Is the worst-case scenario real, or just my perspective (an emotional response)?

She then pinpoints what it would take to fix the problem at hand. If it's a tool or skill she doesn't have, she figures out how to obtain it. Using this approach makes taking on something unfamiliar a challenge to solve instead of a humiliating failure waiting to happen.

Linda's favorite impostor story was of the time she almost got her bough of holly decked one Christmas when she jingled the wrong bell.

A struggling actor in her mid-twenties, Linda was just getting by on a string of part-time gigs, giving piano lessons, teaching music theory at City College of New York, acting in off-off- and more-off-Broadway shows, etc. When the extremely wealthy head of a yogurt dynasty offered fifty dollars—more than half Linda's rent!—to play Christmas carols at the family's annual holiday reunion, Linda grabbed the gig. But there was a problem.

"I was a poor Jewish girl with, shall we say, a limited repertoire of lyrics that included the words 'Jesus,' 'savior,' 'Christ,' or 'Bethlehem,'" she recalls. "But I was a pretty good sight reader and I needed the fifty bucks, so I took the job, and bravely walked inside an apartment so huge it had its own zip code."

The yogurt patriarch turned out to be a formidable man in his early fifties who clutched a baton in one hand and a scotch in the other. He demanded to know if Linda knew all of the thirty-seven carols he placed on the beautiful Steinway concert grand she was about to play.

"Well, not really," Linda answered, a tad too honestly. "But I'm a quick study."

Scrooge McYogurt turned several shades of purple, he was so angry. "He leaned over to me—I can still smell the scotch on his breath—and warned me that if I played just one wrong note, he would bodily throw me out the door."

Linda might have succumbed to the impostor syndrome in that moment and walked out. But she was so incensed by the guy's attitude toward her that she decided to prove her competence instead of questioning her qualifications. And her inner sense of grit served her well. She played not just well, but brilliantly. Not only did she play every note perfectly, but she began to improvise and embellish the music, dazzling the party guests with her impassioned interpretation of each tune. "By the time we got to 'Silent Night,' there wasn't a dry eye in the house. Family members surrounded me at the piano singing with me and asking me to stay long past my allotted time. And the best part? Scrooge McYogurt gave me an extra fifty dollars!"

And she came home with far more than a bulging pocketbook: "What I learned that evening was that even when I took the risk of going out on a limb, doing something I wasn't really qualified to do, I was able to step up to the plate, stretch my limits, and accomplish more than I ever thought possible. Instead of feeling scared, I felt emboldened. I ended up proving to myself that, just maybe, I had underestimated my talents and abilities."

So our advice? When in doubt, ring those bells!

Take a Leap

Robin faced down her own impostor syndrome moment when she was approached in 2013 by a recruiter seeking a CEO to run the American Legacy Foundation, one of the nation's largest nonprofit organizations. Legacy, recently renamed the Truth Initiative, was the antismoking advocacy group that had been established in 1999 as part of the $206 billion Master Settlement Agreement—the largest civil litigation in history between the major tobacco companies, forty-six states, the District of Columbia, and five US territories. The recruiter needed to know within thirty days whether Robin was interested.

Accepting the job would mean dismantling every safety net Robin had. It would mean leaving the advertising industry, where she had focused her professional efforts for her entire career. It would mean leaving a for-profit enterprise for a nonprofit one. It would mean leaving her native New York, her beloved friends, and a career's worth of business contacts for Washington, a city where she knew almost no one. Robin's husband, Kenny, would have to quit his job as a hospital administrator and find a new position in D.C. Everything in her life added up to that one thing we all set out seeking: security. "It was absolutely terrifying to think about leaving all that, to take a step off the edge and challenge myself again."

When the Kaplan Thaler Group had merged a year earlier with Publicis New York, we went from an agency of 250 people to one with 700 employees. Much as Robin welcomed the chance to lead Publicis Kaplan Thaler, she realized that after many decades working in the same business, what she really craved, as scary as it seemed, was the chance to have a "second act," one that would bring an opportunity to learn something completely new and use her years of marketing experience to do something that would have a positive impact on people's lives. Linda assured Robin of her heartfelt support and told her to "go for it."

So Robin picked up the recruiter's letter, and with the deadline a few days away, wrote a passionate response.

Going from selling shampoo to saving lives seemed like an unfathomable leap. On the other hand, Legacy's "**truth**" public education program for teens was legendary. The campaign had won every major award in the ad industry and had been proven to have prevented 450,000 young people from smoking in its first four years. As she drafted her response, it became clearer and clearer to her how strongly she felt about the organization's crusade. She saw herself as twice victimized by the tobacco industry, first as a pack-a-day teen smoker duped by cigarette manufacturers who hid the long-term health effects from the public, and second as a marketer whose entire field was tainted by the money and muscle of Big Tobacco. Robin knew how hard it was to quit—she had stopped smoking for two years and then relapsed, before kicking the habit for good at the age of twenty-eight. Though we had never represented tobacco at the Kaplan Thaler Group, no one in advertising could escape the shoot-the-messenger backlash from consumers who felt horribly betrayed by advertising campaigns promoting smoking.

She finished writing her letter and went to bed. *You know what, Robin, that's probably the end of that,* she told herself. But it felt good to convey how the tobacco companies had made people in advertising look deceptive, manipulative, and dangerous.

"Of course they're going to hire you," Linda predicted when Robin told her what she did. And after a couple of grueling rounds of interviewing, Robin had indeed beaten out more than one hundred candidates and got the job.

Accepting the new position was both liberating and

terrifying, all at once. Peering down into that metaphorical career canyon, Robin steeled herself by flashing back to the toughest question that had been thrown at her during the final interview with the board of directors, when she had been asked how she would feel about running a controversial organization whose rich and powerful foes might well decide to go against her personally. It could, she was warned, get very ugly. Her answer, immediate and straight from her native Bronx roots: "Bring it on."

GRIT BUILDERS

Create your own high wire. Mentally fire yourself. Ask yourself what you'd do if you lost your job today or lost everything you had. Now write a list of the steps you would take. That simple act can take the bite out of the scary aspects of your life if it is upended—because you are mentally prepared. But it can also lead you to be proactive about making a change in your life. The answer may even be the key to your future happiness.

Stop the excuses. An excuse a day makes the goals go away. The next time you make an excuse for something you didn't do or you did badly, turn the excuse into a question. Ask, what could I have done differently? Make a note of it. Then commit to doing it differently the next time.

Make yourself uncomfortable. Get out of your comfort zone. Try getting dressed with your eyes closed, or with one hand. Order something you have never tried before at a restaurant. Say hello to strangers in an elevator. Flexing those muscles will enable you to stick out uncomfortable situations. Research has shown that the brain craves novelty and that doing things that don't feel automatic has a positive effect on neurological activity. It can keep you sharp and can make you more creative.

CHAPTER 5

Get into Wait Training

A handful of patience is worth more than a bushel of brains.

—DUTCH PROVERB

ACHIEVEMENT OF ANY KIND, WE'RE TAUGHT, REQUIRES patience, a willingness to delay gratification. In the space between effort and achievement, between working to accomplish a goal and crossing the finish line, is the waiting: the tedious practice, the endless repetition, the training and rehearsals.

It means clocking endless hours on the treadmill or in the park to train for a marathon, or taking night classes for a year or two to finish that degree you put aside when the kids came along. As excited as you were when you began this endeavor about competing on race day or imagining yourself receiving your diploma on graduation day, those imagined moments of glory remain in the still-distant future. And it often seems harder and harder to stay the course. You become more inclined to reach for a bag of Cheetos instead of your running shoes, or turn on *Game of Thrones* rather than crack your textbook. It's too easy for your mission to be aborted, and your spaceship to be pulled back to earth.

Why does this happen for so many of us, despite our best intentions? It's not because we're incapable. It's because it's hard work. In today's high-tech world, where boredom and our waning willpower can be banished with a mere swipe of our finger or click of a mouse, 24/7, the ability to tolerate tedium or difficulty, practice and repetition, seems to be evaporating by the minute.

Embrace Boredom

This cultural restlessness has become so endemic and alarming to some that Icelandic educator and researcher Margrét Pála Olafsdottir now makes boredom part of the curriculum for the two thousand children in her kindergartens.

Olafsdottir's students are given two opportunities each day to choose which activity they'd like to do for the next half hour. If the children lose interest in whatever activity they have chosen and demand to know what they should do, their teachers resist the temptation to try to recapture their attention. "Great! You're training to be bored! How lucky you are to learn this now!" Olafsdottir applauds them, and reminds them that another chance to choose a different activity will come along soon enough. "Getting bored once in a while teaches resilience," she says.

Learning how to strengthen our ability to delay gratification, it turns out, not only instills self-discipline, it can also make us more creative, flexible, and innovative. As Paul Tough explains in his book *How Children Succeed: Grit, Curiosity, and the Hidden Power of Character,* teaching "noncognitive" skills such as curiosity, self-control, and social fluidity is more likely to result in success than course work that aims to improve intelligence alone. An experiment supporting this thesis unfolded in the mid-1960s, as social scientists recruited three- and four-year-olds from low-income families just outside of Detroit and placed them at the quality Perry Preschool. The idea was to do an educational intervention in an effort to help these kids get ahead. The students were paired with a control group that had no intervention, and both were tracked for decades. While the Perry students' IQ scores had a short-term boost, over the long term those scores fared no better than the control group. However, the Perry students *were* more likely to graduate from high school, land jobs, and earn a decent living than their control group peers. It turns out that the softer skills the Perry students had learned—including self-control—were surprisingly beneficial.

We all know how difficult self-control can be. There is an innate human preference for instant gratification; most people opt for a $20 gift today rather than $100 in a year. Called temporal discounting by psychologists, this phenomenon explains why we feel more mentally invested in what's happening right now than we do about the future, which may or may not come to pass. Temporal discounting also helps to explain why we binge-eat, impulse-shop, and don't save enough for retirement.

Yet there are ways we can manage our impulses, even if we were not taught to do so as children. Linda has a trick that she uses when plowing miles uphill on her treadmill every morning. She sets the exercise machine at the highest incline, 15 degrees, and then, every three minutes, lowers the incline one degree. This literally makes her workout go downhill from the get-go, giving her an added incentive to finish her session. Why quit when the going gets easier? Robin has her own method for resisting instant gratification. At the end of a long day at work, when she would much rather take a cab to her apartment than get home on foot, she makes herself walk for two blocks first, or until she's counted to two hundred. In that relatively short time, the urge to jump in a cab usually passes, because she is that much closer to her destination and has begun to enjoy the walk.

At work, both of us rely on an accountability partner to help us stay on track to meet a goal. We have each found it much easier to meet client deadlines (as well as personal ones, such as writing this book) when working as a team, because neither wants to be the drag who's not doing her share.

Of course, we never know if we will be successful in an endeavor when we first set out. In fact, some of the more accomplished artists and crusaders in history never got the chance to bask in the glory of their achievements. In the nineteenth century, when American women had little opportunity to get an education, and married women were considered the property of their husbands, Susan B. Anthony envisioned a day when both men and women would have equal say in shaping society. Branded a dangerous renegade, Anthony spent fifty years relentlessly fighting for women to win the right to vote. "Failure is impossible," she insisted in her last public speech as a suffragette, a month before she died at the age of eighty-six. Her spirit and determination never wavered, despite the obstacles in her path. Fourteen years later, in 1920, her dream was finally realized when Congress enacted the Nineteenth Amendment to the Constitution, giving women the right to vote.

The genius of artist Vincent van Gogh has amazed generations of art lovers. But van Gogh was little known during his life and toiled in poverty. He sold only a single painting before his death at age thirty-seven. Yet his passion and grit helped him to create more than two thousand works of art in his short career.

Three years after architect Robert Mills submitted his winning design for a six-hundred-foot Egyptian-style marble obelisk to be built in Washington, D.C., the cornerstone of the Washington Monument was laid on Independence Day in 1848. But politics and budget concerns—although this took place more than 150 years ago, it was still Washington, after all—halted construction six years later, when the monument was only 156 feet high. Mills died the following year, his beautiful monument an unfinished eyesore.

It wasn't until twenty years later, when the US Army Corps of Engineers took over the project, that the Washington Monument was finally completed.

Our point? Think of how diminished the world would be if these individuals had tossed in the towel when their dreams were stymied. What each of them had in common—what so many people of great accomplishment share—is grit: the guts, resilience, initiative, and tenacity to persevere in the face of setbacks, even when their dreams and goals seemingly disappeared into an uncertain future. Nevertheless, there was nothing plodding or dull about their efforts. In fact, just the contrary was true—their unquenchable passion and endless zeal gave them the grit to persevere despite the odds.

When Robin was interviewing at Legacy (now the Truth Initiative), she met the man who has become a legend in legal circles and nonprofit organizations: Mike Moore. Moore was the initial driving force behind the epic legal struggle to hold tobacco companies accountable for the millions of deaths and devastating illnesses their addictive products caused in this country. Moore's personal and professional grit became the stuff of law journal legend, resulting in a landmark ruling that has literally saved millions of lives. It is also a shining example of how a passionate belief in one's goal can empower you to wait years before it comes to fruition.

Turn Passion Into Perseverance

Moore was a county district attorney fresh out of law school; he spent a decade building his reputation as a tough-on-crime Democratic prosecutor, before being elected attorney general of Mississippi. When Moore was a few years into the job, Mike Lewis, a law school classmate from the University of Mississippi, came to him in the wake of a friend's agonizing death from lung cancer, with a radical proposal: What if the state took on Big Tobacco? Individuals devastated by smoking-related disease had been trying to hold cigarette manufacturers accountable for more than forty years—ever since the *British Medical Journal* first linked smoking to cancer in 1950 (followed by the US surgeon general's report in 1964 drawing similar conclusions). But the tobacco industry beat back every lawsuit and attempt at legislation, arguing that smokers had free will and were responsible for their own actions. And juries agreed.

Profoundly moved by his chain-smoking friend's terminal lung cancer, Mike Lewis had an *aha* moment. He suggested a new legal strategy: What if the state sued Big Tobacco to recover the taxpayer money spent on Medicaid to treat patients with lung cancer, emphysema, and other smoking-related illnesses? Moore, Lewis, and a third Ole Miss alum spent a year studying the issue and drafting a strategy for taking on the tobacco industry in what was certain to be a David versus Goliath, years-long battle. Mississippi, after all, was one of the poorest states in the Union, and Big Tobacco had billions of dollars in its war chest, as well as a legion of aggressive lawyers with decades of experience beating back courtroom challenges, and a well-honed strategy of delays and appeals.

"It sounded like a fool's mission. It wasn't that I thought necessarily that we'd win," Moore told us. "I thought we could file the case and tell the American public the truth, and expose the industry's big lies: that cigarettes don't cause cancer, that nicotine is not an addictive drug, and that they don't market to children. I knew I was doing something for the right reason." Moore knew it would be a long, hard legal haul with little hope of victory. Nonetheless, they filed the suit on May 23, 1994, and held a press conference to tell the tobacco industry point-blank: "You caused the health crisis, you pay for it." He was immediately ridiculed by Mississippi's Republican governor. Then he was ordered not to spend a single penny of taxpayer money on the litigation, or use any members of his staff on the case. When he asked the federal government to join in the suit, he was told he didn't have a case. The message from both state and federal government, and the tobacco industry, was loud and clear: you're on your own.

"At our first hearing, it was the three of us and sixty-three lawyers from the tobacco companies," Moore recalls. "That's when I knew: I gotta build a bigger team." He began approaching other state attorneys general in search of allies. By the end of 1994, three states had become part of the suit. By 1996, there were seventeen on board. Tobacco industry lobbyists responded with their own campaign. Moore started getting hate mail from farmers and Chambers of Commerce all over the country. "I absolutely thought I could lose my career." But the lawyers taking on the tobacco industry were determined. One of the co-counsels, Moore remembers, drained his savings and mortgaged his house to help fund the fight; Big Tobacco, meanwhile, was spending an estimated $600 million a year defending itself. Although it took four exhausting years, Moore ultimately triumphed, when Big Tobacco agreed to a settlement totaling hundreds of billions of dollars to forty-six states, the District of Columbia, and five US territories in the Master Settlement Agreement. (The other states, including Mississippi, brokered separate agreements.)

"Determination is going to keep you going a lot longer than money or adoration," Moore told us. It is a truism we learned firsthand from our work with health-care companies.

Celebrate Small Victories

In advertising, our longest, toughest projects are often our assignments for pharmaceutical companies. We would often come on board while a drug was still in Phase 3 clinical trials. Often this means two years of work before the drug has even a hope of getting into the marketplace—assuming that the drug is finally approved. We have worked on any number of new drugs for a year and a half or more, only to learn that the drug did not receive approval by the Food and Drug Administration. Years' worth of hard work can get shut down in days. Keeping teams motivated during that long ramp-up period requires that people stay focused on the long term—which is especially challenging when their peers within the agency are celebrating shorter-term campaigns, rewards, and recognition. Often, to sustain motivation, this means celebrating smaller victories, such as a good meeting, a favorable advertising test score, or a shout-out from the client in an earnings report.

Robin faces these same long-term challenges working on the **truth** campaign, today. In 2014, she helped to lead the launch of a major reinvention and reinvestment of **truth.** Robin knew it would take an enormous amount of grit for those on staff to give 110 percent to a project that wouldn't be declared a victory until the final research results were delivered in 2017 (when a ten-thousand-person longitudinal survey measuring the long-term impact of the campaign on youth smoking would be complete). Because of that long wait for gratification, it was vital to celebrate smaller victories along the way to keep motivation high. Every week she sends a weekly email to the staff to call out small measurable achievements, such as an increase in the number of views of the campaign's YouTube videos, Facebook likes, or sign-ups at the website. It's a practice we made part of the culture at Publicis Kaplan Thaler, and one of the reasons we were always as intent on pursuing smaller pieces of business as well as the trophy fish. Pitching the relatively small NAPA Auto Parts account, for example, not only flexed our creative muscles while we were getting ready to pitch a mega-account like Wendy's, but also provided a nice dose of job-well-done in the meantime.

"Working on multiple projects simultaneously in a sense

staggers gratification," says architect John Mack, a design partner at the award-winning firm HLW International. Among HLW's portfolio is the renovation of the prestigious United Nations Secretariat Tower in New York. The renovation took over eight years with multiple consultants, working closely with the UN staff to complete work on the breathtaking 505-foot-high skyscraper that forms the centerpiece of the UN headquarters in New York City.

"It's difficult to work on a project for that long and maintain the high level of commitment it deserves," Mack admits. You need to always keep the end product in mind as well as learn to celebrate the small victories. "That may be approval of a design, reaching a construction milestone or most importantly for me the excitement of seeing a space begin to take shape and knowing you've made the right decisions."

David Gal and Blakeley B. McShane, assistant marketing professors at Northwestern University, found the same thing to be true when they looked at one of people's most common long-term goals: paying off debt. After studying random data from some six thousand consumers who had turned to a leading debt-reduction firm for help, the professors found that those with an achievable goal were more likely to settle their accounts than individuals who saw a long, hard road in front of them with little hope of rewards or other payoffs before the finish line. While the conventional wisdom says you should pay off your highest-interest debt first, paying off a credit card with a low balance—even if the interest rate is low—is so encouraging that it makes the consumer more likely to pay off other debts. Essentially, these small victories create a snowball effect. "When pursuing a long-term goal, people should focus on checking items off their list, rather than focus simply on making progress toward their goal in an absolute sense," the professors suggested.

Appreciating the motivational value of smaller accomplishments helps to develop the endurance you need to tackle bigger, long-range goals. As those of you who knit might know, it is better to knit a perfect row and pause to admire your work than to think about the entire sweater and how much you have yet to do. Civilization came about because, at some point, our ancestors developed the patience to sit for hours rubbing two sticks together.

It is that same degree of grit and determination that makes the Navy SEALs so effective on dangerous missions.

Make Your Bed

When US Navy admiral William H. McRaven returned to his alma mater to deliver the commencement address to the Class of 2014 at the University of Texas at Austin, he shared the lessons he learned from his SEAL training. His number-one lesson—making your bed—was a surprise to the entire audience, given the notoriously tough six months of basic training recruits face to become a Navy SEAL. Candidates must conquer punishing obstacle courses, midnight swims in the cold Pacific Ocean, sleep deprivation, and routine ten-mile runs with full packs and enough calisthenics to leave them blistered, bruised, and sick to their stomachs. They're constantly drilled by officers whose mission is to find the grittiest members for each class, and weed out the weak, the unwilling, and the recruits who simply give up.

"Every morning in basic SEAL training, my instructors, who at the time were all Vietnam veterans, would show up in my barracks room and the first thing they would inspect was your bed. If you did it right, the corners would be square, the covers pulled tight, the pillow centered just under the headboard and the extra blanket folded neatly at the foot of the rack—rack—that's Navy talk for 'bed.'

"It was a simple task—mundane at best. But every morning we were required to make our bed to perfection. It seemed a little ridiculous at the time, particularly in light of the fact that we were aspiring to be real warriors, tough, battle-hardened SEALs. But the wisdom of this simple act has been proven to me many times over. If you make your bed every morning you will have accomplished the first task of the day. It will give you a small sense of pride and it will encourage you to do another task, and another and another.

"By the end of the day, that one task completed will have turned into many tasks completed. Making your bed will also reinforce the fact that little things in life matter. If you can't do the little things right, you will never do the big things right. And if by chance you have a miserable day, you will come home to a bed that is made—that you made—and a made bed gives you encouragement that tomorrow will be better. If you want to change the world," the admiral advised, "start off by making your bed." If making your bed is a great way to start the day, here's a great way to end it.

Robin has a daily ritual that helps her to put a positive spin on each day and set the stage for the next. She is religious about cleaning her desk each evening. No-longer-needed documents and notes get tossed, emails get filed, and folders are sorted into stacks of "urgent for tomorrow," "priority," and "can wait until later." It means she needs to stay at work longer at the end of a hard day but it serves to underscore the day's accomplishments (even when it feels there may have been more setbacks than progress) and it sets the stage for an optimistic start to the next, when she can dive right in to what needs to be done with a fresh perspective.

Set Small Goals

Taking the measure of a person's grit is a more accurate barometer of how successful he or she will be than any report card or résumé. Your sense of grit shows you have the stick-to-itiveness and determination to accomplish your goals—that your character offers more than meets the casual eye. Educator and consultant Michael Motto developed a keen sense of a potential student's grit when he was an admissions officer for Yale University.

Sorting through thousands of college applications from Ivy hopefuls revealed a great deal to Motto about the students who felt privileged and entitled, versus those who had a genuine hunger to succeed. Texas, for example, was one of his favorite areas of the country, because it encompassed a demographic that included the richest of the rich, and the poorest of the poor. In the Rio Grande valley, the competition to get in to Yale was stiff among the bright Mexican American kids the Ivy League colleges particularly coveted. Motto remembers one applicant named Julio who came from a blue-collar family. Getting admitted to an Ivy League college was Julio's dream in life. He had strong grades, Motto recalls, but his test scores "were not so good." He had some interesting activities listed on his résumé, but he wasn't a standout like some of his Texas competition. Yet Julio applied early, and emailed Motto every week for months. He was deferred, which at a highly competitive school like Yale meant he was unlikely to get in. So he emailed Motto again. "If you allow me, I want to keep you posted on everything I do," Julio wrote. Motto tried to politely dissuade him with the standard reply, "We have all the information we need and will get in touch if . . ." etc. But Julio continued to write anyway. His dream of getting into Yale might have been a long shot, but he refused to give up. So he set himself a series of smaller goals to improve his chances, reaching out to local judges, landing an internship with one of them, and becoming a passionate volunteer in a local reading program.

"There was something about this kid I had not seen," Motto realized. "He had a vision for himself. He wasn't the product of some consultant or coach. He had this desire to do everything within human limits to accomplish his goal." And it worked. Ultimately, Julio was admitted to Yale. He went on to win competitive fellowships for overseas research and travel and, last Motto heard, was pursuing a career in New York.

He achieved his goal not in one giant step, like several of his classmates who segued seamlessly from high school academic success to the Ivies, but by reaching toward the finish line one step at a time.

It's not easy to persevere when we don't know how long we have to wait, or whether or not our imagined future will ever come. It's why those signs in train stations that tell you when the next train will arrive are so comforting—just knowing that makes the wait less torturous. But even when the trains run on schedule, there can be derailments along the way. Dealing with them may force us onto a new track. And that could be a good thing.

GRIT BUILDERS

Doing nothing is doing something. The next time you are waiting at the dentist's or the doctor's office, or for a train or a client, resist the urge to take out your phone and check email or Facebook. Be still. Notice the world around you. Think about what you are feeling. What in your life are you hungry or thirsty for? It's in these moments of boredom and inactivity that we can be our most creative, solve problems, engage with the world around us, and train ourselves to accept that we don't always have to feel busy to be fulfilled.

Be a list lover. Robin practices this approach every Sunday night, when she hones her weekly to-do list, a chore that often interferes with watching the latest episode of *Homeland* or *The Walking Dead*. Making the list not only reminds her what she needs to focus on in the coming week; it also gives her a little jolt of satisfaction as she realizes how much she accomplished the prior week—as well as gives herself the pleasure of crossing things off her list. The act of deleting an item, especially those that she has carried on the list for a while, helps make the Sunday night blues less onerous, and allows her to face Monday with a positive attitude.

Lose your willpower. Research has shown that willpower only works for a short time. It's the reason most of us make our dieting vows on January 1, and then go back to eating brownies and hot fudge sundaes two weeks later. Changing behaviors that tempt us on an hourly basis takes an enormous amount of energy, energy that gets readily depleted as the day wears on. A better strategy is to create a new behavior, and repeat it over and over, until it becomes an automatic, subconscious response. For example, instead of being tempted to text a friend while you're driving, get into the habit of throwing your phone into the backseat when you get into the car, so that there is no way for you to reach it. And that hot fudge sundae that kid is scarfing down in the restaurant booth next to yours? Don't fight the urge to dig your spoon into it. Instead, visualize an army of ants climbing into the bowl. Works every time!

Hit the thirty-second pause button. In advertising, half a minute can be long enough to change someone's mind. But it is not so long that it feels interminable. That thirty-second pause can be enough time to counter negative impulses from steering you down the wrong path—whether it's doing something you shouldn't (like eating that second helping of pie) or preventing you from what you should be doing (such as practicing the violin). So if you feel an urge to indulge in a guilty pleasure, pause. Count to thirty. You may find the impulse will fade, and you can carry on with your work.

Be grateful. A recent study in *Psychological Science* found that one key to self-control can be as simple as cultivating gratitude. Thinking about what we *have* puts us in a positive mood, which in turn helps us make better choices. Conversely, negative moods make us more impulsive. So the next time you find yourself about to make a hasty, spur-of-the-moment financial decision, like splurging on that expensive bottle of wine at dinner instead of paying off your Visa bill, hit pause, and remind yourself to be thankful for all you have. In that brief moment, you'll probably realize that a less expensive bottle will taste perfectly fine. Your credit rating will thank you, too.

Chapter 6

Bend Like Bamboo

Nature has a funny way of breaking what does not bend.

—Alice Walker

Eleanor Longden was hearing voices. At first they were simple, neutral narratives describing what she was doing in that moment as a student at the university she attended—leaving a seminar or opening a door. The voices were so real that she would look around for their source. When she realized the dialogue she experienced was internal, she sought medical attention. She was diagnosed with schizophrenia, a mental disorder that, among other things, makes it hard to distinguish between what is real and what isn't. Doctors prescribed medication for her, as is standard practice, but the voices grew more persistent and menacing, encouraging her to dump water on a teacher, which she did. Ultimately, Longden felt so trapped and became so despairing that she tried to drill a hole in her head to let the voices out.

The diagnosis could have been the beginning of a long spiral into institutionalization, life on the street, or even suicide. But there were two people instrumental in Longden's life who elevated her situation above the ordinary. First, there was her mother, who believed that somehow Longden would make it through, and repeatedly told her so. And second, her doctor, who helped her understand that the voices only reflected metaphoric examples of her own fears. When a voice would tell Longden not to leave the house, she came to learn how to deconstruct the meaning behind that voice, seeing that what it was really saying was that she was afraid. And once she understood better what was happening in her mind, she was able to confront her fears, and the voices backed off. Longden practiced these mental exercises for years, slowly regaining her ability not only to function, but to thrive.

A decade after her schooling was interrupted by the voices in her head, Longden was able, finally, to finish her studies, earning a PhD in psychology—yes, the voices dictated some of the answers to her on her exams—so she could help others like her. She is now a board member at a global support and research organization that is helping to spread positive messages about the experience of hearing voices. She has turned what seemed to be a disability into an asset—a sixth sense. To many, Longden may appear a tower of strength. She withstood sexual abuse in both childhood and adulthood, not to mention schizophrenia. For most of us, any one of those might be enough to cause us to retreat or shrink from the world. But contrary to popular wisdom, Longden's ability to turn enormous obstacles around is less about having the strength of a sturdy oak and more about having the flexibility of a slim stalk of bamboo that bends rather than breaks in the wind. In fact, the humble bamboo may be the perfect metaphor for the resiliency that is one of the critical components of grit.

Despite its hard body, bamboo is incredibly flexible, thanks to its hollow interior. It will sway even in the gentlest breeze. Yet it will often be the only thing standing after a typhoon, its roots firmly anchored. Bamboo plants can endure challenging temperature extremes of winter and summer, and yet they are one of the fastest-growing plants in the world. Unlike other woods used in making furniture, bamboo doesn't need much finishing—it's ready to use as is. There are arguably many life lessons to glean from bamboo, such as learning to face obstacles not with stubborn resistance, but with the flexibility and confidence of knowing that you can adapt to change.

Of course, flexibility and adaptability are essential elements of grit. We live in a world where innovation and change are accelerating at a pace never before seen. Business plans are no longer written for the next five years, and when they are written at all, chief executives must be willing to rip them up at any time. How we react when faced with a shifting landscape—from handling a more challenging assignment at work to a critical situation in our personal lives—is affected to a large degree by our sense of grit. It affects how we deal with setbacks big and small, and the mistakes of others.

Ultimately, if you're always bent in the same direction, how can you see the sky full of opportunities that are open to you?

Surviving by Improvising

We all face challenges in life, whether they are physical, emotional, financial, cultural, or circumstantial, such as just being in the wrong place at the wrong time. That was the situation for Linda's French cousin, Edith Weill, during World War II, when Weill, her husband, and her three children were sent to a Nazi internment camp in Drancy, outside Paris. From there they were about to be put on a train to Auschwitz when a French policeman recognized her. He explained that if she told the Germans they were Christian and only half Jewish, they would be allowed to stay. She quickly fabricated an elaborate story. When a Nazi official demanded to see her papers, she lied, and claimed they had been destroyed in their hometown of Guerling. She specifically chose Guerling because she knew there would be no records left, as the town had been destroyed by the Germans. The Drancy camp's second in command, known throughout the camp as the Butcher, interrogated Weill for months, hoping to catch her in a lie about her Jewishness. But she remembered every detail she had made up and recounted it faithfully for three years, and in doing so was able to keep her family alive until the French liberation.

Longden and Weill are vivid examples of our natural innovativeness, resilience, adaptation, and flexibility under the most extreme adversities. But our need for grit and resilience does not require a life-or-death situation. Sometimes, love and longing can push a person to the limits of what seems possible.

There Is Always a Way

Malvern Hoyt, the oldest of six children in his family, left his home in Benson, Nebraska, after graduating from high school. It was the last thing he wanted to do, but his parents simply could not afford to pay for his upkeep, now that he had finished school. So, at the age of seventeen, he set off—on foot—to find work wherever it was available. After twelve years of struggling through odd jobs across the country, he landed work as a bouncer in a Boston nightclub. But one snowy December day, missing his family after so many years away, Hoyt decided to travel back to Benson for Christmas, even though home was 1,400 miles away and there were only four days until Christmas.

His friends thought he was crazy. Without a car, or even a driver's license, and no money for a cross-country bus or train, Hoyt started out on foot on December 21, a particularly cold and wintry Boston day. He hitched rides when he could, but often had to walk several miles between rides. At one point he walked across the entire city of Cleveland before hitching his next ride. Making his way west without sleep, or shelter, he got as far as Chicago on December 24.

He was still a long way from home, but he refused to give up on reaching Benson by Christmas. Hoyt was able to catch a ride on an automobile transport truck that took him as far as Joliet, Illinois. But he was still almost five hundred miles from home. Through the kindness of strangers, he was given a free room at a local hotel. Christmas Day, Hoyt began hitchhiking again; with the few dollars he possessed, he boarded a bus, which took him, finally, to Benson. From there Hoyt walked a half mile through the snow to his family's home. When he walked through the door at 6 p.m., the entire family was just about to sit down for Christmas dinner. Their tears of joy at Hoyt's almost magical appearance were all Hoyt needed to convince him that his passion and determination had been worth it.

Why is it that some people, like Malvern Hoyt, have the grit and determination to succeed against all odds, while others do not? Research shows it's not about having nothing to lose; rather, it's about believing there is much to gain. In other words, grit speaks to our capacity for hope—and whether you see the world through the lens of a glass half full or a glass half empty.

Sunny Side Up

Arthur's son was taking care of his weekly chore of mowing the lawn when the family's riding mower started to make an awful banging sound. Arthur, alerted to the racket, stopped what he was doing to inspect the metal shroud covering the mower blade. But as he touched the machine, the twisted blade came to life and sliced off his three middle fingers. Arthur was an electrician by trade, so his hands were his livelihood. With the EMTs on their way, Arthur frantically searched for his fingers. He found two of them before he was rushed to the hospital.

A hand surgeon was able to salvage some of the ring finger (less on the middle and index fingers) and restore some sensation. But Arthur was devastated, afraid he'd never be able to work again. The doctor reassured him that he'd be fine, over time—most of a hand's strength, the doctor told Arthur, comes from the thumb and pinkie. In other words, the fingers he lost were the ones he could best afford to lose.

The doctor's optimistic words were critical in helping Arthur reframe his reality as he recuperated. He slowly regained dexterity, and eventually went back to work. Over the years, he became a highly respected foreman, motivating and inspiring his crew with his tireless work ethic, positive attitude, and self-deprecating sense of humor. In fact, today, when anyone on the job asks if he needs a hand, he deadpans: "No, but I could use three fingers!"

"You make the best of it," Arthur now says cheerfully. "It's amazing how adaptable and resourceful the human body is."

Of all the ways in which Arthur adapted to his missing three fingers, learning to be optimistic was perhaps the most crucial. And yet, the notion that optimism can be learned seems surprising. Isn't optimism an innate quality? You're either born with a sunny disposition or you're not, right?

Psychologist Martin Seligman of the University of Pennsylvania has studied the power of optimism for decades. His research suggests that optimism (like pessimism) is a quality that each of us can learn. Seligman was part of a research team in the 1960s involved in giving mildly painful shocks to dogs, rats, mice, and cockroaches, to test their resiliency. Eventually the animals realized they had no control over when and whether they received the shocks, so they began to accept their inevitability, without attempting to escape. Seligman and other researchers conducted similar kinds of experiments on humans. In this case, participants, divided into three groups, were forced to listen to loud music. Those in the first group could press a button to stop the overbearing sound. Those in the second group could not turn off or turn down the music, though they tried repeatedly. Those in the third control group were given no music to listen to at all. The next day, when each of the subjects was presented with noise, all they had to do to make the sound stop was move their hands a few inches. Those in the first and third groups figured this out quickly. But those in the second group, who had been conditioned to feel powerless over stopping the loud music, did nothing. Seligman and the other psychologists called this reaction "learned helplessness."

Surprisingly, however, over the course of many such studies, psychologists discovered that about a third of the animals and people in such learned helplessness situations do *not,* in fact, come to feel helpless. Why? Seligman believes the key is optimism. Hundreds of studies have confirmed that pessimists—those who believe that negative events are long-lasting and out of their control—are more prone to resignation and depression, essentially stifling their incentive to work their way out of a bad situation. Conversely, optimists—people who view setbacks as temporary conditions that they can overcome or transform—are more motivated to solve their problems. They tend to perform better than their experience or natural ability might otherwise suggest. At heart, optimists believe they have the ability to change their circumstances—that with hard work over time, they can overcome challenges and setbacks.

This, of course, has huge implications. Think about how effective a pessimistic salesperson would be. After a few weeks or months of unsuccessful cold-calling, they would tend to give up, or at least approach the next call or sales lead with far less enthusiasm. College students who receive a poor grade in a class might conclude they just aren't smart enough to do well, or aren't any good at the subject, and switch majors, or even quit school. In sports, a lack of personal or team success might extinguish a budding athlete's desire to play (rather than instill a determination to work harder to develop their strength, speed, or skills). In each case, the individual's talent or aptitude is often less important than their attitude—their sense of optimism, and their drive to work harder to get better.

The good news is that optimism can be learned. According to Martin Seligman, the building blocks of optimism include positive emotion, engagement, and meaning—developing your unique strengths and skills toward an end bigger than yourself. Longden, over time, acquired all three of these optimism building blocks. "Having these meaning-ful relationships [with individuals] who believed in me and my humanity and my capacity to heal was very important," she told us. "When the time was right they were able to—I say they saved me, but they did more—they gave me the power to save myself."

Failing Forward

Optimism is essential in being resilient; it allows us to stay motivated during trying times. But failure can be an equally powerful force in driving us to work harder. In recent years, failure has become an area of intense study in busi-ness schools, and a badge of honor among the fiercely driven entrepreneurs in Silicon Valley. There is even a magazine called *Failure,* which serves as a resource for those trying to succeed. Indeed, failure today is often seen not as something to be embarrassed about, but as one of the keys to learning faster, being more creative, getting better, and ultimately finding a way to win and succeed.

We have experienced this firsthand so many times. You lose again and again in the highly competitive world of ad-vertising, whether in a pitch, or even the chance to pitch, not to mention losing desirable accounts or key members of your team. Taking hits like that can be emotionally devas-tating, especially for creative people who pour so much of themselves into generating new ideas.

Over the years, when we'd lose a big business pitch, we'd give the staff the bad news—often face-to-face—in a short, sweet, and matter-of-fact manner. "Unfortunately, the client selected Leo Burnett" (or whatever competitor had won the account). Then we quickly focused on the positive, talking about the quality of the ideas we had come up with and the many new clients we would now be able to pursue as a result of the work we'd done. Rather than drag the bad news out, whining or rationalizing over the reasons for the loss, we'd end the conversation with three simple words—"We move on." Such meetings are always about resetting our optimism and converting negative energy into a force for positive change.

Countless successful people acknowledge the importance that failure played in their lives. Oprah Winfrey was demoted from her first job as a news anchor because her boss said she "wasn't [built] for television." Rather than giving up, being fired gave her the grit to prove her boss wrong. Dr. Seuss, one of the biggest-selling authors of all time, had his first book rejected by twenty-seven publishers. Lady Gaga was dropped from her first record label three months after signing. And Abraham Lincoln, America's greatest president, failed in business, and was defeated in eight previous elections before winning the presidency.

Imagine failing more than a thousand times at something. Or three thousand. How many of us *wouldn't* give up? Well, meet James Dyson. Dyson failed more than five thousand times as he struggled to create his first Dual Cyclone vacuum cleaner. He finally brought it to market in 1993, fifteen years after his initial effort. The British inventor has since been knighted and runs a multibillion-dollar company known for its innovative and forward-thinking designs. He claims that failure "is part of making progress. You never learn from success, but you do learn from failure. [When I created the Dual Cyclone vacuum], I started out with a simple idea, and by the end, it got more audacious and interesting. I got to a place I never could have imagined because I learned what worked and didn't work." With each successive failure, his idea was reshaped, reborn, and, ultimately, evolved into a brilliant groundbreaking invention.

One of the tenets of world-famous economist Albert O. Hirschman was that failure is a powerful force for innovation and resourcefulness. In other words, it can serve as the mother of creativity. In order to truly develop grit, he would argue, we need to embrace the gift of failure. Dyson was able to view each failure as a step toward ultimate success. Learning to turn failure or frustration around is certainly difficult. One way to make the process less painful is to practice reorienting your point of view, and see the situation from another perspective.

Turn Your Telescope Around

A couples' counselor we know has an unusual but surprisingly effective method for helping her clients work to repair their broken relationships. She believes that we get so used to looking at the world through one set of lenses that we become blind to other possibilities. So she uses a technique that forces her patients to view the world through an entirely different angle, by "turning the telescope around."

When a couple on the verge of a breakup comes in, she asks them to work jointly to come up with five good reasons for cannibalism. Of course, defending eating another human is ludicrous; what the exercise teaches couples, however, is to work collaboratively and approach their problems from a different perspective. Before they know it, two people who could not even agree on the price of milk are suddenly working together to come up with answers like "a good source of protein" and "end overpopulation." And they realize that they have more in common than they thought when they walked in the door.

Changing our perspective can help us view many of life's challenges differently—and that is especially true of failure. When our friend Joel Kweskin was downsized in the prime of his career as an insurance executive, he indulged his hobby as an amateur cartoonist, bringing his art supplies to parties and creating caricatures of the guests. Joel had always been a gifted sketch artist, but he had never considered the possibility that he could refocus his career around his drawing talent. The reaction to his cartoons and caricatures was so positive, people began hiring him to draw them at political functions, corporate affairs, and social events. Years later, Kweskin realized that losing a job he merely liked freed him to enjoy a career he now cherishes.

But how do you turn your life around when you've lost all hope?

EVELYN WYNN-DIXON'S BLEAKEST moment came in 1973 when she was standing on a bridge overlooking Atlanta's

Interstate 75, preparing to jump. She had dropped out of college when she got pregnant. Then Wynn-Dixon had three more children. Now a single mother without a job or the ability to feed her family, Wynn-Dixon thought that committing suicide would allow her kids to collect on her insurance policy and make them rich. As she watched a tractor-trailer approach the bridge she was standing on, she realized, "I am not gonna be able to do that." So she went home, instead, where she had a .22-caliber pistol. But she discovered she had no bullets. She tried overdosing on aspirin and cutting her wrist, but her spirit—and her body—refused to give in.

After her unsuccessful suicide attempts, she remembers hearing her late mother's voice telling her to turn her life around by going back to school. So she did. She first earned a nursing certificate, then a bachelor of science, then a master's in social work and gerontology, and eventually, a PhD in public health. She walked the many miles from her home to her classes, and paid tuition and supported her children through cooking and cleaning.

In 2007, at the age of fifty-eight, she ran for mayor of Riverdale, Georgia. She won—the first of two terms—and is still serving as of this writing. Her constituents say she has been a tireless ambassador for Riverdale, bringing the city together at a time of surging crime, changing demographics, and economic challenges. Not only has she turned her own life around and improved the city, but her children all attended college; one went on to earn an MBA from Harvard.

She says now about her decision to change her life, "It was the fact that I dared to get up. I kept saying, 'This is not going to defeat me. I'm going to prove to people that I can make it.'"

Grow Your Mindset

Wynn-Dixon changed everything about herself. For others, reinvention—as well as resilience—is a way of life. It's certainly true of Danny Flamberg. After graduating from college with a dual degree in religion from the Jewish Theological Seminary and political science from Columbia, Danny became an ordained rabbi. Discovering a dearth of synagogues where he could find employment, he decided to use his training, and his ability to see myriad sides of any given issue, to earn a PhD in econometrics at Columbia. That helped him secure a job as a foreign affairs/defense producer on the *MacNeil/Lehrer Report* (turning down an invitation from a former professor and the CIA). When the show hit a funding crisis, Danny used his newfound media and communications skills to move into the public relations sector, where he restaged the Mutual Radio Network and introduced America to Larry King. When the network changed hands, he took his newly honed marketing skills to talk his way into a position as chief marketing officer of 1-800-Mattress. There he dedicated himself to becoming proficient in the burgeoning digital landscape. That later led to a role as CMO of CellularOne. When the franchise was sold, Danny once again found himself jobless. So he launched a career in the advertising world. Our point? After each change of circumstances, Danny landed on his feet, armed with yet more experience, more ideas, and more opportunities. His insatiable curiosity ultimately gained him respect and experience in the digital arena, and today Danny is one of the industry's most respected experts on digital customer relationship marketing (and a member of Publicis Kaplan Thaler's senior leadership).

Asked how he made the rather unlikely journey from leading a religious congregation to landing digital advertising clients, Danny says, "My life has been one long series of zigs and zags. I've always been the kind of person with a natural curiosity and optimism. When something doesn't turn out the way I think it should . . . I'm good at dusting myself off and saying, okay, what did I learn and how can I use that to tackle what's next?"

There's a term for Flamberg's ability to bend, flow, and adapt. It's called having a *growth mindset.*

Stanford University psychologist Carol Dweck believes that people have one of two types of mindsets: fixed and open, or growth. Those who have a fixed mindset believe their intelligence and talent are fixed traits, based on their genetic inheritance. The problem with such a mindset is that when such individuals encounter difficulties, they assume there is nothing they can do about it; after all, they are only as smart as the genes they were born with, so they give up. Even students at the top of their class who have a fixed mindset struggle when they encounter a challenge they can't master. They assume they simply aren't smart enough to solve it. Those with a growth mindset, however, refuse to give up in the face of adversity or challenge. They believe their abilities can be developed through dedication and hard work and focused practice or attention. As a result, those with a growth mindset are not cowed by obstacles. Rather, they see them as challenges to be overcome. It's a view that, according to Dweck, "creates a love of learning and a resilience that is essential for great accomplishment. Virtually all great people have had these qualities."

Wynn-Dixon and Flamberg clearly are growth mindset people. So is Jim Abbott, the Major League Baseball pitcher who, in the 1990s, played for the New York Yankees and Chicago White Sox, despite being born without a right hand. When he was a child, he would throw the ball at a wall with his left hand, while holding his glove in his partial arm, and then seamlessly switch his glove to his throwing hand before the ball bounced back to him. In order to learn how to do this more rapidly, he would first practice from farther back, and then move closer and closer to the wall. As a major-league player, Abbott went on to pitch a no-hitter for the Yankees.

Haskell Wexler is another growth mindset person. In 1966, he won an Oscar for black-and-white cinematography for the award-winning film *Who's Afraid of Virginia Woolf?*, starring Elizabeth Taylor and Richard Burton. He won a second Academy Award for cinematography in 1976 for the film *Bound for Glory,* a full-color biography of Woody Guthrie. These awards are acknowledgment enough of Wexler's talent with a camera, but they are even more impressive when you discover that Haskell is color-blind, unable to see reds and greens properly. Wexler suggests he may have compensated for his sensory loss by paying more attention to light, a feature that is obvious in his work in such movies as *In the Heat of the Night,* starring Sidney Poitier, which won an Academy Award for Best Picture. The 1967 film was the first major Hollywood production shot in color featuring an African American star.

Wexler lit the film in an unusual way. He enhanced existing lighting sources—using airplane landing lights instead of car headlights—and ignored the popular tonal range of color. In essence, he brought a black and white sensibility to a color film, which was not common then.

Like others with grit and an open mindset, Wexler refused to be stopped by his disability or to be cornered by obstacles.

SHELDON YELLEN FACED a different kind of adversity. Growing up in Detroit with an absent father and a mom who relied on welfare, Yellen and his three brothers were forced to start working at a young age to scrape by. For Yellen, that meant washing dishes five days a week in a hamburger shop when he was only eleven, giving his mother his pay. When he was promoted to wait tables, and received his first tip—one dollar!—he was so excited he dropped a dime in the pay phone and called his mother to tell her the news. She hung up on him, irate that he had just wasted 10 percent of his tip.

When Yellen got married, his wife's brothers asked him

to join the family business, which had started as an awning company with an office in Dearborn, Michigan. Many of the twenty employees looked at him like a charity case— the family hire. "Nobody talked to me or helped me," he recalled with a chuckle. To break the ice, he'd write each of them a personal birthday card, knowing that relationships were an important key to success. Through a lot of hard work, which he'd embraced from a young age, he helped transform the business into a company that sells disaster relief repairs to insurance companies. Today, the company, Belfor, is a $1.5 billion enterprise with more than 6,400 employees. And he continues to send birthday cards to every one of them.

Create High Expectations

Research shows that Yellen's mom, with whom he remains very close, unwittingly did him a great favor by pushing him to be independent and strong as a kid. Dr. Kenneth Ginsburg, a professor and pediatrician at the Children's Hospital of Philadelphia who specializes in developing resilience among young people, believes kids *need adults who believe in them unconditionally and hold them to high expectations.* Children need to feel competent and confident, Ginsburg says, by being given opportunities to develop important skills, and by being allowed to recover themselves after a fall. They need to develop a clear sense of right and wrong and a commitment to integrity. And they need to learn coping strategies and self-control to help them get through failure or times of pressure and stress. What we do to model healthy resilience strategies for our children, he claims, is more important than anything we can teach them or say to them.

We met Yellen in 2012, as he and Belfor restored a school in Henryville, Indiana, that had been destroyed by a deadly tornado. The company had promised the community it would complete the work in five months, to open on time for the first day of school. It was an audacious schedule. But they met their promise—others estimated the project would take two years—by working seven days a week. Their crew saved a library full of yearbooks from the rubble and even rescued one of the classes' goldfish, caring for it until the school reopened. Yellen's grit and perseverance have become part of the DNA that flows through the Belfor culture.

In retrospect, perhaps it is not surprising that negative experiences—fear and anger in the case of Longden, repeated failure in the case of Dyson, color blindness in the case of Wexler, adversity and hardship at an early age in the case of Yellen—can become positive influences, as they force us to dig deep within ourselves out of sheer necessity. But positive influences, too, help us develop grit in our lives: gratitude for what we have, an innate sense of generosity, and a desire to give something back to society. Such influences can strengthen our sense of grit through the simple act of doing a job well that we enjoy, and that motivates us to be our best.

Yellen's work in disaster recovery—and his approach to helping others—are a reflection of where he has come from and what he has accomplished in his own life. He asked the people of Henryville to look at tragedy and adversity as the *beginning* of a process of recovery, not the end. He tells younger employees, including his two children, who work at Belfor, managing up to twenty jobs at a time, that success is a journey, not a destination. "Enjoy the path," he says. "Look around you. It's not a dash."

That resilience in the face of adversity is the essence of bamboo. Although it may grow slowly at times, and slowest of all in the dead of winter, it's constantly finding a way to reach for the sky, sometimes saving its greatest growth efforts for times when conditions and circumstances are right. That can happen at any stage of life.

GRIT BUILDERS

Embrace Plan B. Sometimes it can even be more effective than Plan A. When Steven Spielberg's mechanical shark malfunctioned on the set of *Jaws,* he used music as a stand-in, creating a lurking underwater menace that was even more terrifying than the shark we could see.

Recharge your spirit. When you've had a disastrous day, give yourself a break in order to gain a fresh perspective on a problem, or muster the strength to fix it. And sometimes, of course, you just need to go to bed. Sleep, as Arianna Huffington points out in *Thrive,* has a restorative function, washing toxins from the brain and improving reasoning, problem solving, and attention to detail.

Setbacks move you forward. On average it can take as many as eleven attempts to quit smoking before someone is finally able to stop. But each time you fail, there is something you can learn about how to succeed the next time. Take the time to examine how each setback can propel you forward. Then get back up and try again, and again, and again.

CHAPTER 7

No Expiration Date

Age wrinkles the body. Quitting wrinkles the soul.

—GENERAL DOUGLAS MACARTHUR

JAMES HENRY GREW UP POOR IN THE AZORES. HIS FATHER forced him to quit school in the third grade to work odd jobs. Eventually, Henry moved to Connecticut and became a fisherman. What no one knew was that he was illiterate— something that he hid with clever tricks, such as waiting for others to order at a restaurant so he could say, "That sounds good," without having to read the menu. But illiteracy finally caught up with him late in life when his family gave him legal documents to sign about where he was going to live. It was a situation that caused a lot of hurt feelings and animosity.

At the age of ninety-two, James spent months hunched over the kitchen table, learning the alphabet, practicing his signature, and slowly progressing to reading simple children's books. Then his wife died, sending him into a tailspin and robbing him of his motivation to learn to read. But his story doesn't end there. At the age of ninety-six, Henry became determined to try to learn to read again. This time he not only dove back into reading, but, with the help of a retired English teacher, he began to write, longhand, about his life, his time at sea, a man he lost overboard on one voyage, and what his grandfather's farm was like in the Azores. He finished his memoir, and when he was ninety-eight it was published and became a bestselling book called *In a Fisherman's Language*. It was optioned to become a film, and his success triggered a congratulatory letter from President Obama. Henry was working on his second book when he died at age ninety-nine in 2013.

Henry's story is remarkable on many levels. First, it took a tremendous amount of grit just to get by in today's world as an illiterate adult. Even more remarkable was his determination to overcome it later in life.

Grit Is Age Agnostic

Yet perhaps we shouldn't be so surprised by Henry's accomplishments as a nonagenarian. Emerging science tells us that most of the cognitive limits we think we face as we age are self-imposed. The brain is like a muscle that, with exercise, gets stronger. And its plasticity and growth are fueled by learning new tasks, creating new memories, and taking on new challenges. This is true whether you are eight months old or eighty years young. It's only when we don't use our intellect that it begins to waste away.

Ruth Hamilton blogged well into her 109th year, and George Weiss, whose eighty inventions had all been rejected by companies, at the age of eighty-four created an award-winning word game called Dabble, which today is sold nationwide. The same is true for pushing the limits of our physical selves. Chris Moon, who, at thirty-three years of age, lost his lower right arm and leg while clearing land mines in Africa, went on to complete, less than a year later, in the London Marathon and has become a prolific ultra-marathon runner as well as a motivational speaker. Speaking of the personal grit it takes to make the impossible possible, he says, "What happens most of the time is that we stop . . . at this point at which it hurts a bit too much. But the reality is that we have the capacity to go beyond that point if we believe we can. If you fall over, keep on getting up."

We would also argue that sometimes, even with physical challenges, perseverance and drive can trump a more youthful capacity for physical endurance. Diana Nyad, at sixty-four, after four unsuccessful attempts when she was in her twenties, pushed the limits of human exertion in 2013 by swimming for fifty-three hours straight, from Cuba to Key West, Florida, in waters infested with sharks and jelly-fish. Her resolve and determination grew stronger when she felt the ticking of her biological clock. How long was she going to wait to accomplish a goal that had haunted and inspired her most of her life? she asked herself. The grit required to train for months, and to pull herself through the pitch-black Gulf waters at night, unable to see what lurked below, vomiting seawater at several points, dehydrated, almost delirious at times, was amazing. Her advice upon finishing? "Don't ever give up. You can chase your dreams at any age. You're never too old."

What we love about these stories is that the individuals did not abide by the conventional wisdom about age and accomplishment. As a society we are fixated on "use by" dates and time limits on pursuing our goals, regardless of how old we are. We look sideways at people who keep trying to achieve a goal well past the time when most people think enough is enough. Yet many of these supposed Johnny- and Jenny-come-latelies apparently never got the "too late to be . . ." memo. Ken Jeong, an internist turned comic (*Knocked Up, The Hangover*), began his acting career when he was almost forty years old. And Sethanne Howard (who just retired from her position as chief of the Nautical Almanac Office at the US Naval Observatory) didn't receive her PhD in astrophysics until she was fifty. Perhaps one of the most extreme examples of ageism is the story of ballerina Misty Copeland. At the tender age of thirteen, when Misty decided she wanted to be a ballerina, she was actually considered too *old* to pursue a dance career. Yet through years of exhaustive practice and a belief that she could succeed, Copeland, at thirty-two, is an internationally celebrated soloist with the American Ballet Theatre. All of these stories, and so many more, are proof positive that the only limits we have are those we place on ourselves.

The Overblown Under-Thirty Hype

Our culture is an impatient one, in love with youth and the idea of getting rich quick or quitting Harvard to found Facebook. In a recent Havas Worldwide report, 63 percent of global consumers feel our obsession with youth has gone over the deep end, with the pressure and stress to achieve something earth-shattering in our twenties paralyzing millennials into believing they are losers before they have even begun their careers. With a plethora of "thirty under thirty" success stories, is it any wonder this generation feels like they've failed before they've even begun?

Yet we are robbing ourselves, no matter what age we are, of the tenacity, and years it may take, to finally succeed. And precisely because it goes against the cultural norm of "making it" when you're young, it takes even more grit to start a new endeavor for the first time later in life. (Heck, we were in our forties when we founded the Kaplan Thaler Group, despite advertising supposedly being a young person's business!)

In fact, if you plot the ages when creators released what became extraordinary successes, the dots are all over the map. But we tend to focus on the fact that Picasso was able to churn out amazing paintings when he was twenty, even though he created some of his most daring work in his eighties. The truth is it's a better story to talk about the six-year-old piano prodigy than the sixty-year-old playing at Carnegie Hall.

If you don't start training in a sport before age seven,

the thinking goes, why bother; you'll never be an Olympian, or win a Division 1 college scholarship. If you don't finish college in your twenties, or if you have not launched your career by the time you are thirty, you're a bust.

But that is a social invention. It's bunk. If you are willing to put in the work, the truth is, almost any goal, at just about any age, is within your reach.

Go for the Gold

Genevieve Damaschi was an orphan during the Depression. She lived in a foster home that overlooked a pond where kids flocked to skate in the winter. She was a talented dancer, and while she longed to learn how to spin and jump and tango on ice, she had no money for skates. After Damaschi got married, she became busy raising three daughters. It wasn't until she was in her early forties, when her youngest moved out of the house, that she was finally ready to take the ice. She'd be at the rink at 5 a.m., the first one there and often the last to leave. She listened intently to her world-class coaches, completing training drills alongside the Olympic hopefuls. And she began competing. She did not care that she was the oldest skater out there, and relished being a maternal figure, boarding and cooking for the teenagers at training camp in the summer. Her hard work, and imperviousness to time and age, paid off. Within a decade she won a national gold medal for mixed-pairs ice dancing with a sixteen-year-old partner. Although the gold medal was not an Olympic one, Damaschi did win on Olympic ice (Lake Placid) in an Olympic year (1980), which made the whole accomplishment that much more special. She was fifty-two.

So what are some things you can do to keep your grit growing and going strong? First, you need to maximize your mind.

Pump Up Your Brain

Remember the fable of the race between the tortoise and the hare? Grit—hard work and determination—is like the winning tortoise, while sheer talent and youthful ability is the hare. And we all know who won that race. Here is an example. Science now shows we weren't born with all of our brain's gray cells; we can grow billions more later in life, regardless of age. But the way to do so is through giving our brains demanding tasks throughout our lives. Hard work stimulates renewal and growth at the neurocellular level. For example, those with learning disabilities, such as dyslexia and attention deficit disorder, often have to work harder to learn new things. But this can be a long-term advantage, helping them to keep intellectually engaged throughout their lives, feeding their creativity and making them stronger visual, conceptual, and spatial thinkers. It can also make them late bloomers, in a society that tends to overvalue instant success.

Our brains crave novelty. Regular stimulation of all the senses and activities like nonroutine actions and thoughts encourages growth of new neurons and the branchlike dendrites that extend from them. Until recently, scientists thought dendrites only grew in children. And scientists have found dendrites can atrophy if they are not used. But they can also grow at any age if they are stimulated properly. Based on this, Manning Rubin and Lawrence Katz, authors of *Keep Your Brain Alive,* argue that simply brushing your teeth with your nondominant hand—activities Katz calls "neurobics"—can go a long way in slowing down the aging of the brain and keeping it healthy. Neurobics include exercises using various combinations of the physical senses—touch, smell, hearing, taste, and sight—in novel ways. Our brains are constantly reorganizing, stretching, and making new neural connections. (It's why training platforms such as Lumosity.com exist—to sharpen memory and problem solving.)

Neuroscientists reveal that while cognitive decline starts in our twenties, physical exercise can help slow that decline. Someone who is smart, engaged, and active in his or her sixties or seventies can score higher on cognitive tests than a couch potato who is half their age.

Today we know that even exercising for twenty minutes can facilitate information processing and memory functions. That is because aerobic exercise increases heart rate, which pumps more oxygen to the brain and helps to release hormones that encourage the growth of brain cells. Exercise also creates new connections between cells of the brain. That runner's high we've all heard about? The same antidepressant effect from running is also associated with increased cell growth in the hippocampus, an area of the brain responsible for learning and memory.

Some types of exercises can improve cognition even more. Ballroom dancing, an activity that makes both physical and mental demands on dancers, can have a greater impact on cognitive functioning than exercise or tasks that challenge our brain functions alone. Why? Because such physical neuro-workouts involve and integrate different parts of the brain used in coordination, rhythm and balance, and strategy.

Don't Act Your Age

Too many of us tend to believe the hype that age defines and limits our potential. As consumers and viewers, we naturally tend to imitate what we see. But a study conducted by psychologist Ellen Langer, which in 2010 was replicated in a reality BBC show, *The Young Ones,* had some age-defying results that show that people act according to their environment. Six aging celebrities spent a week at a house that was renovated, from carpets to couches, to look like a home in 1975, a period when most of them were in their twenties. Their clothes were from the 1970s as well. In other words, there was nothing in their environment to remind them that they were over sixty. After one week, the impact on the six celebrities was incredible. One of the actors, who had come in a wheelchair, was able to walk with a cane, and another who could barely put on his socks was now able to dress himself without assistance. Langer's earlier study also revealed that blood pressure decreased, manual dexterity increased, and even their sight improved. Just turning the clock back in our perceptions may actually help us to regain some of the stamina, endurance, and strength we had when we were younger.

Keep Moving

Science suggests that the best path to sustaining physical and intellectual achievement is to never hit a stop sign. A basic law of physics states that a body in motion tends to stay in motion. In fact, we chose those words as a part of a slogan for a campaign we created for a drug that helps relieve osteoarthritis pain. The research showed that when people are afflicted with arthritis, they tend to move less, because movement is painful. But movement actually helps to ease the pain. By taking this drug, they could move more easily and thereby stay more active. We tell that story because it is a great metaphor for the process of achievement throughout life, especially for those who are starting "late." With regular challenging work that exercises and strengthens our body or mind, our physical and intellectual abilities can remain vibrant and strong, as well. And without it, they can wither.

Imagine if society were more accepting of the belief that success can come at any age. Would we have more Picassos and Diana Nyads if, as a culture, we didn't decide that people who are beyond a certain age are washed up, and past their due date? The fact is we live longer today than ever before in human history. So why not use our capacity and our grit to fulfill not just one goal, but perhaps several over a lifetime?

As former Paramount Pictures CEO Sherry Lansing likes to say, why should we ever think about retiring, when we could be "rewiring"?

Retire Retirement

Retirement is another cultural idea that may lead people to give up career and life goals years before they might actually want to stop working. Shouldn't we be encouraging each other to keep going, to cure cancer, to win a Nobel Prize, or to discover a new planet, solar system, or galaxy? Is there any magic to reaching the age of sixty-five? There isn't. Retirement was invented by a nineteenth-century German chancellor in response to rising Marxism in Europe. The fact is, it was not created because older people were incapable of doing good work, but rather because young people wanted their jobs at a time when there were not enough jobs to go around.

Furthermore, older workers are not less productive. Using the economic standard measure of worker productivity—hourly wages—those between 60 and 74 are 10 to 20 percent *more* productive than their average younger counterparts. They also score high in leadership, detail-oriented tasks, organization, listening, writing skills, and problem solving, even in high-tech fields. Researchers at the University of Mannheim in Germany looked at teams of workers at a BMW plant. Productivity increased right up until the mandatory retirement age of sixty-five, because these veterans knew how to handle problems and prevent mistakes.

Clarence Nicodemus was a biomechanical engineer and director of spine research at the University of Texas Medical Branch at Galveston. He spent seven years there working alongside orthopedic surgeons, exploring how the spine functions and developing instruments to repair spine damage. As a result of his work, he became interested in finding nonsurgical ways to treat back pain—something he claims surgeons were not focused on. So, at the age of fifty-seven, he set out to become a doctor, taking the MCAT and applying to roughly forty medical schools. He was rejected by all but one. But one was enough. He graduated in 2004 at the age of sixty-one as the oldest student ever from Michigan State University College of Osteopathic Medicine.

"My definition of retirement is doing what you want to do, and this is what I want to do," he said.

Be a (Re)inventor

Marvin Kaplan, Linda's dad, is an inventor. He was originally educated as an electrical engineer. Early in his career he developed a patent for some of the internal wiring for the first television sets, then created the precursor to the electric fence, followed by developing radar used to help paratroopers during the invasion of Normandy in World War II. When he retired in the mid-1980s as vice president of manufacturing and electronics engineering at CBS, his biggest question was "What will I do next?"

After he and his wife, Bertha, Linda's mom, moved to Delray Beach, Florida, he invented things to help his friends, such as better hearing devices they could use in their retirement community's theater, and giving classes to his fellow residents on how to convert their home movies into digital videos, as well as lecturing monthly on topics ranging from robotics demonstrations (he designed the Maxx Steele robot for CBS) to advances in Lasik surgery. He taught residents to use soldering irons and small tools. He devised and taught the residents how to make things such as an electronic painkiller, and a fake car alarm.

Today, at the age of ninety-five, Marvin and Bertha are living in an independent living facility in New Jersey, where Marvin has reinvented himself yet again. When he asked his fellow residents how their everyday lives could be improved, they told him they wanted to laugh more. So he organized a comedy workshop for them. He finds the funniest clips on YouTube and presents them in one-hour "laugh" seminars. He redid all of the wiring in the meeting room so that attendees could easily watch the clips from wherever they were sitting. With boundless energy, he has become a star in his community. If you want a good chuckle, take Marvin's class.

Marvin has been a doer and a problem solver his whole life because he is passionate about invention. And it gives him joy. Loving what you do can make you more productive, sociable, and innovative. That kind of enjoyment can help fuel the grit needed to help us persevere when we face the inevitable challenge.

The Encore Effect

Marc Freedman founded Encore.org, a platform to connect the growing cohort of older workers and employers in second, and perhaps third and fourth, acts that benefit society. Freedman claims people want to work as they near, or even surpass, what he believes is an outdated retirement age, and employers recognize the hard work and dedication they bring to the job.

Spurred by wanting to make a difference, people in their fifties, sixties, seventies, and eighties are fighting poverty and environmental challenges and working on the streets with the homeless. "They are all tackling tough issues in a sustained way. None of these problems can be solved with a quick burst of insight. They are also stories of ups and downs and failure. And they go at it again and again. You don't have to get everything right," Freedman says.

In a recent survey, Encore.org found that there are 9 million people in the United States who are in encore careers and another 31 million who claim it's a priority to them to find an encore career. Some colleges and universities, including Harvard, are building on this idea, encouraging older workers to take classes or be part of research groups—and they are getting a great response.

Seventy-five percent of those eligible for retirement say they are staying on the job not because they need the money, but because they enjoy what they do. For them, work helps to keep them mentally engaged and physically fit. But as we will see in the next chapter, we can turn our natural grit into an amazing force for doing good.

GRIT BUILDERS

Do the math. We all have limited time in our days and lives. But ironically, the less we have, the more we are able to focus on what truly counts. Make a list of pluses and minuses at the end of each day. Tally them up. If the minuses outnumber the pluses, you've got an opportunity tomorrow to do better.

Say no to "not yet." While it's good to plan, don't wait until the stars are aligned perfectly to take advantage of opportunities that pop up in your life. A "not yet" mindset can make you feel less energized and more resistant to change. What are your "not yets"? Is there a step you can take now toward tomorrow?

Have a hundred-year plan. We are living longer and working longer. In fact, the fastest-growing age bracket globally is those in their 100s. Establish a series of life goals for every five or ten years of your life. Think of the things you'll have time for as you pass key milestones; prioritize the things you want to accomplish at different stages of your life.

CHAPTER 8

Grit for Good

Happiness is not the absence of problems. It's the ability to deal with them.

—BEHAVIORAL SCIENTIST STEVE MARABOLI

PRIMITIVE HUMANS, TRYING TO SURVIVE ON THE HARSH savanna, learned some important lessons the hard way, including that cooperation was essential to staying alive. In foraging communities, if one person hit the jackpot on a berry bush, she'd share, so that next time, when her search for food came up empty, her group would share back with her. In the end, by working hard not only on our own behalf, but also on behalf of others, we all lived to fight another day.

These behavioral patterns, which have evolved over millennia, have become so ingrained that they are part of our evolutionary psychology. Altruism is not why we cooperate;

we are altruistic, according to a growing consensus, in order to survive. We developed these collaborative skills on a larger scale, making us "group-minded" and allowing us to identify with others even if we don't know them personally.

What that means is that our brains are hardwired to do good. Our deepest source of motivation comes from a desire to help others. And a growing body of scientific research argues that the act of helping another person triggers activity in regions of the brain involved in pleasure and reward; helping others is like gratifying a personal desire. In one study of macaques, scientists found "that although a monkey would probably never agree that it is better to give than to receive, they do get some reward in a specific brain region from giving to another monkey."

Through human evolution, these "moral" behaviors remain an essential part of who we are—it is why people were able to summon unsuspected courage and run toward the explosions to help strangers during the Boston Marathon bombing, and why doctors and nurses risk their own lives to help fight Ebola. And this is really good news, because what it takes to make the world a better place requires a great deal of hard work—long hours, little to no pay, sometimes toiling in harsh environments at great risk, with little measurable success in sight. It is our gratification, appreciating the smallest success, that motivates us to keep going in these circumstances, regardless of whether or how much we get paid. In fact, the harder the problem, the more satisfaction we feel trying to solve it. Research published in 2012 in the *Journal of Consumer Psychology* called this phenomenon the

Ikea effect: shoppers value a piece of furniture more if they have to put it together.

A Hunger to Help

Navyn Salem was no expert on hunger and malnutrition, outside of the three meals plus snacks she fed her own four young daughters as a stay-at-home mom in a comfortable Rhode Island suburb. She had a communications degree from Boston College, marketing experience, and a father who had emigrated to the United States from Tanzania—a country that she described to us as "an oasis of peace, surrounded by conflict and turmoil and very high rates of severe acute malnutrition."

Salem believed in the saying that from those to whom much has been given, much is expected. And so, wanting to combine her business background with her interest in children and personal connection to her father's homeland, she went to Tanzania to research opportunities. While there, she was inspired by a factory that employed three thousand local women to make mosquito nets to prevent malaria—solving poverty and public health issues simultaneously. She thought it was a great model. Later, back home, she saw a *60 Minutes* segment on a product called Plumpy'Nut—a vitamin- and mineral-enriched peanut-based paste that doesn't require water or refrigeration and helps feed and bring back to life severely malnourished kids younger than five years old. And a lightbulb went on.

In 2007, she sent Nutriset, the French inventors of

Plumpy'Nut, a letter suggesting they partner with her to open a factory in Tanzania. Half the ingredients were already available in the country (including peanuts and sugar). But she got no immediate response. She tried again, but still no answer. A couple of months later, Nutriset agreed to meet with her. She won them over with her passion, enthusiasm, and determination to help create a sustainable social enterprise in Tanzania.

Next, Salem steeled herself for the challenge of overcoming the tangle of red tape within the Tanzanian government to develop national guidelines for the use and distribution of ready-to-use therapeutic foods, and to start pilot programs in several regions. Boiling down that sequence of events to a sentence belies the years of hard work and seemingly endless problems she faced. Just because she wanted to solve the global crisis of childhood malnutrition, starting in Tanzania (with about 20 million children with severe acute malnutrition globally), didn't mean anyone was waving a magic wand to help.

"I knew it would not be easy but there was no way to know precisely what roadblocks would have to be overcome," she said. Getting nonprofit status was a challenging eighteen-month process. Figuring out how to create a start-up staff based in Dar es Salaam was hard. Learning all the stakeholders and the politics; how to get things done from such a long distance; how to find land and figure out who owns it; how to understand the legal implications of her work—there were new problems to solve every day.

"I had a one-year-old, a two-year-old, and six-year-old twins. I spent every waking moment that I was not changing diapers or driving to ballet on this project. Probably twenty hours per week in the beginning and then up to forty-plus hours once it started to take off." Typically she would start work when she put her kids to bed at 7:30 p.m. and go until she collapsed with exhaustion. In 2009, after stepping back from the East African factory to let it be run by local Tanzanians, she established Edesia in Providence, R.I., as a non-profit, where products are sold at cost to large humanitarian partners. Working full time without any compensation, Salem's Rhode Island factory has helped prevent and treat malnutrition for over two and a half million children in over forty-four countries. Having an achievable goal enables Salem to stay motivated, despite how daunting the crisis of childhood malnutrition is.

BEING PART OF a web of programs, services, and individuals committed to solving the issues of our time requires a special kind of dedication. It's not about being famous or taking credit for an achievement. It's about plugging away at a cause, especially if the problem isn't going away. It's using your grit, whether to help others halfway around the world or right where you live.

Develop Your Character

It's certainly a plus that we have these natural tendencies. But is that enough? How do we instill the type of character in ourselves and others that makes people willing to dedicate themselves to creating a better world?

Schools and parents are typically focused on instilling practical skills they think children need to be successful. But there are some in education who embrace *character building* as a foundation for success. The motto of KIPP, a national network of college preparatory public schools in underserved communities, is "Work hard. Be nice."

They are words Leticia Van de Putte and her siblings were taught to live by as a family of Mexican descent growing up in Texas. They were taught at an early age what it means to live a life of significance in one's community; that it's never really work if you are doing something you are passionate about, especially if it helps other people. Van de Putte's grandfather owned a pharmacy and he worked seven days a week, making sure anyone who was ill had the medicine he or she needed to get by. When the entire family would go away to the beach each year for a long weekend, he refused to go. When Van de Putte asked him why, he'd point to the pharmacy and say, "Why would I want to leave this? My whole life is a vacation." Van de Putte also became a pharmacist, as well as a mother of six, adding to her large extended family. Growing up, she experienced discrimination—her father, a US military veteran, was denied the purchase of a home because of the deed restrictions against Latinos in the neighborhood he sought to live in.

And she learned firsthand in pharmacy school that women had to work harder than their male colleagues to get ahead. Wanting to help children, women, minorities, and small business owners, she ran for political office. Elected to the Texas legislature in 1990, she served her constituents while still filling prescriptions.

But 2013 was something of a personal crucible. Since January, political tensions had been running high across the state due to a bill that would restrict a woman's right to choose an abortion. In May, the youngest of her six grandchildren succumbed to sudden infant death syndrome. He was just five months old. A month later, her father, one of the guiding forces in her life, was killed in a car accident. Then her mother-in-law died.

On the night of her father's burial, while she was at a family gathering watching a memorial slide show of him, a historic filibuster led by close colleague Senator Wendy Davis was unfolding at the state capitol to block a bill that would make legal abortion more difficult in the state. Her chief of staff pulled Van de Putte aside to tell her what was happening, as pictures of her father smiled down at her from the screen at the funeral reception. "It hit me how many times my dad was there for me. How many times he stood up for me as a woman, as a Hispanic. It just clicked. I looked at my staff and I said I had to go." She arrived on the Senate floor around 8:30 p.m. exhausted, unaware the event had gained national attention. She ended up igniting an explosion of sustained cheers and applause from the gallery. (The filibuster she was part of played a major role in delaying passage of the bill beyond the midnight deadline for the end of the legislative session, although it ultimately passed in a second session.)

Not long after, the incident turned into a groundswell of support for her to run for other offices. As of this writing, she had resigned her state senate seat to be a candidate for mayor of San Antonio. Her desire to give back to her community provided her with the grit—or *ganas,* the Spanish word she uses for *grit*—that drove her to carry on.

It isn't hard to see that Salem and Van de Putte love their jobs, even as they toil away. Serving others can increase the dopamine coursing through our brains, the chemical that makes us happy. It can raise our self-esteem and our sense of well-being. A 2013 review of forty international studies suggests that regular volunteering can add years to your life— with some evidence pointing to a 22 percent reduction in mortality, according to study coauthor Elizabeth Lightfoot, an associate professor at the University of Minnesota School of Social Work. No matter how old you are, helping others can help yourself: a study in *JAMA Pediatrics* found that even high school students saw a drop in their cholesterol levels after volunteering with younger kids once a week for two months. In adults, those over fifty who volunteered at least two hundred hours in the past year (roughly four hours per week) were 40 percent less likely than nonvolunteers to have developed hypertension. Even completing five small acts of kindness (like helping a friend, visiting a relative, or writing a thank-you note) one day a week for six weeks created a significant boost in overall feelings of well-being. And the effects are cumulative. Imagine the benefits of working full-time for decades helping others.

Get Back Up

Most people are surprised to discover that hard work can be the key to personal happiness, as well as its own reward. In fact, many argue that happiness cannot be pursued; it comes about as the unintended side effect of one's personal dedication to a cause greater than oneself. Psychologists call it the *happiness paradox*.

It was a lesson that Trevor Houser learned the hard way.

Linda first met Trevor Houser at City College of New York (CCNY), in Harlem. His story, she realized, embodied the full arc of potential for someone, through the power of grit and perseverance, to climb out of a hole in life, not just to better their own situation, but to make a difference in the world.

Growing up in Wyoming, Houser bounced around between divorced parents. His family lived off welfare for a time while his mother finished school and searched for jobs as a physical therapist. Houser fell into drinking, drugs, theft, and "other shenanigans." He dropped out of high school in his junior year, and worked as a busboy at a restaurant. He lived a "pretty small life without a lot of prospects." Then he got arrested, facing substantial prison time for things he'd done while he was under the influence of drugs.

But the district attorney in his hometown told him he could avoid prison by getting treatment and making restitution. And that's what Houser decided to do. Living in Portland, Oregon, he landed a job at a call center for an Internet service provider, helping older customers learn how to get online. He taught himself graphic design skills and was looking for a job in that field when a recruiter reached out to him about a graphic design job at a large bank in New York City. Just nineteen, Houser moved to Brooklyn. But he was laid off not long afterward when the dot-com bubble burst in 2001. So he went back to working as a busboy in an Italian restaurant in Park Slope, Brooklyn, and as a butcher's assistant at a meat counter next door.

It was hard, physical work. He'd come home from those jobs hungry for intellectual stimulation, and read the *New York Times* every day, from cover to cover. Drawn to international economic issues, he earned his high school equivalency degree and applied to the closest academic program he could afford: CCNY, where he became a Colin Powell Leadership Fellow. In the course of his studies, he realized the importance of China in the global economy and applied for a State Department internship in Beijing for the spring of 2004. But before he left, Houser was diagnosed with a brain tumor. He had successful surgery and spent six months recovering, delaying the internship until the following year. Once at the US embassy in Beijing, he was placed in the environment, science, technology, and health section of the embassy. The department was desperate for research assistance, sending him into Mongolian coal mines, exploring the oil and gas fields in Shandong Province, and meeting with environmental activists.

He returned to New York and, during his senior year at City College, was given the opportunity to take a couple of classes at Columbia, where he met Professor Daniel Rosen, a China expert. Houser became Rosen's research assistant, and eventually his coauthor and business partner at Rhodium Group, a global consulting agency that deals with energy and environmental topics. The Obama administration recruited Houser to help deal with one of the most vexing issues of our time, climate change. As a senior advisor to the State Department, Houser negotiated seven bilateral US-China energy agreements in 2009, and was a member of the U.S. delegation at the UN climate change summit in Copenhagen that year.

"I remember sitting there in a room in Copenhagen with twenty-five heads of state and thinking this is a pretty long way to come from cutting up pork shoulder and washing dishes," Houser told us.

But there was a reason, of course, he was there. And it had to do with opportunity, grit, and giving back. "I had been given three second chances I didn't deserve. So I feel like I owe it to the people and institutions that invested in me to prove it was the right decision to make, and my responsibility to give back and try to make those same opportunities available to others wherever I can."

HOUSER WAS ABLE to triumph over his personal setbacks and challenges, and ultimately use his unique intellectual gifts to help work on an ever-greater global challenge. Perhaps finding a way to conquer his own difficulties growing up helped to instill in him the grit he needed later in life to take on something as daunting as the world's climate crisis.

As the research of psychologist Angela Duckworth shows, those who are challenged physically, emotionally, or economically early in life are often more driven to succeed later in life. And for some, overcoming those personal challenges can help to nurture a deep empathy for others and the desire to help. That was the case with Houser, as it was with another person who has an incredible degree of grit, Brian Bob.

Give the Gift of Grit

Brian Bob, who struggled with reading difficulties as a young man, has devoted his life to helping disadvantaged teens. For the last twenty-five years, he has worked at Covenant House, a youth homeless shelter, where counselors use their grit 24/7 to help kids get their lives back on track. But there's one story that still brings tears to Bob's eyes.

Early in Bob's career, at a Covenant House in Los Angeles, he met a nineteen-year-old we'll call Ray, who was addicted to crystal meth. Like many others his age living on the streets, Ray came from a troubled home. He had joined up with a group called the Trolls that lived under the 101 freeway; sometimes they would squat in abandoned buildings. Bob and his team would try to help Ray get cleaned up and sober. Ray would come to Covenant House for a time, and then go. It became a pattern. One chilly evening, Bob found Ray lying on the street, bleeding. Ray once again asked for shelter. It was a hopeless cycle; Ray just did not seem motivated enough to turn his life around.

Realizing that Ray was destined to return to the streets after yet another stay at Covenant House, Bob decided to try a different approach. He took Ray in the Covenant House van to the local Skid Row, where porta-potties and fire pits signaled the public's tacit acceptance of this permanent homeless community on the streets of downtown Los Angeles.

"I thought we were going to Covenant House!" Ray cried out in confusion.

"No, no. We're kinda done with that. This is where you're going to end up anyway, so why don't we just do it now?"

Ray got out of the van in a white tattered shirt and bawled. As Bob attempted to leave, Ray begged for mercy. So Bob took him to Covenant House, hoping that the tough-love message would stick, but doubting whether it would permanently change his behavior. Soon after, Bob relocated to a Covenant House in Oakland, California, and never found out what became of Ray. Then, ten years later, Bob got a call from the Covenant House in Los Angeles, saying someone named Ray had just stopped by and asked for him. On hearing Ray's name, Bob assumed that he was still an addict and living on the street.

"Oh my God, what kind of shape was he in?" Bob asked. The L.A. director laughed.

"He looked pretty darn good," Bob heard through the

phone. "In fact, he just gave Covenant House a check for ten thousand dollars."

Ray *had* turned his life around. He had started his own successful construction company. In donating to Covenant House, he was hoping to help others from landing on Skid Row. Ray's parting words: "Please tell Bob that the day he took me to Skid Row is the day I swore off drugs forever."

Bob still works at Covenant House. And now he endeavors to pass on his sense of grit and determination to others, to help turn their lives around. He has helped to change the lives of thousands of young kids over the years.

People like Navyn Salem, Leticia Van de Putte, Trevor Houser, and Brian Bob are trying to help make the world a better place for us all. Whether or not they solve world hunger, climate change, or homelessness, they have each found a way to make a difference, and brought others into the solution. Salem's factory workers in the United States and Tanzania are now among the beneficiaries. Despite political setbacks, Van de Putte remains dedicated to serving her largely Latino community in San Antonio. Trevor Houser's work has gone global, giving governments a framework for implementing change. And Brian Bob keeps working to stem the tide of homelessness, one kid at a time.

GRIT IS THE great equalizer in life, because anyone, at any time, whatever their background or resources, can lay claim to it. It's been proved time and again, that those individuals who relentlessly and passionately summon their inner fortitude when things get tough or scary; who tirelessly turn defeat into victory thanks to their resilience; who turn roadblocks into initiatives; and hold on with the fierce tenacity of a mother tiger to her cubs, are the true winners in life.

With grit, there's no telling how far you can go, how much you can do, or how successful you can be.

So what are you waiting for?

GRIT BUILDER

Google for good. Looking to be a part of social change? Want to be a volunteer or find a paid position that will help make the world a better place? If you're unsure where to start, there are lots of websites you can explore, such as VolunteerMatch.org, Idealist.org, or AllFor Good.org, which connect interests and the amount of time you have to spare with organizations that would love your help. It's a good way to test if the work is a match for you—and do some good while you're at it.

Join the grit movement. For more information, please visit www.grittogreat.com.

Acknowledgments

A HEARTFELT THANKS TO TINA CASSIDY, OUR WONDERFUL writer, researcher, and collaborator. Your spirit and enthusiasm are infectious and we are so very appreciative of your talents in bringing *Grit to Great* to the finish line. To Kristina Grish and Tamara Jones, thank you for your help with finding and interviewing so many amazing people for our book.

Thanks to Richard Abate, our astute and visionary literary agent at 3Arts Entertainment, who is always on the pulse of what will fascinate and engage readers, and whose wise counsel has proved to be invaluable over the last several years. A big shout out to his trusted assistant Melissa Kahn, who helped to expedite the arduous journey along the way.

Roger Scholl, at the Crown Publishing Group, has been our talented and dedicated editor for our last four books. Roger, your advice and commentary never fail to make every page better. A special thanks to the entire team at Random House, including Megan Perritt, publicity manager; Ayelet

Gruenspecht, marketing manager; Rachel Berkowitz, associate subsidiary rights director; Cathy Hennessy, production editor; and Heather Williamson, production manager. Your valuable expertise in helping us to market and promote *Grit to Great* have been greatly appreciated. And our deepest gratitude to the leadership at Crown Business, Tina Constable, publisher; and Campbell Wharton, associate publisher. A special thank-you to Wade Lucas, agent director at the Penguin Random House Speakers Bureau, whose energies have helped us bring the empowering message of *Grit to Great* to audiences large and small.

A huge thank-you to Liz Hazelton and Allison McLean, the literary marketing and public relations gurus at Amplify. Your expertise and out-of-the-box thinking has helped to put *Grit to Great* on the short list for "must reads" and we cannot underscore how grateful we are for your wisdom and insights. A huge cyber "bravo" to Ken Tola and Mac Cassity for their creative talents promoting our book in the digital and social media arena, and a special thank-you to Rachel Davis for all her social media help during the launch of our book. Not an easy task, but your experience in this area has proven invaluable. To the exceptionally astute and talented Tricia Kenney, who has been the mastermind publicist behind so many of our books, thank you once again. You never fail to find the glitter in whatever we set out to do. And a big hoorah to Erin Creagh, who helped with our Grit talks, presentations, and whose infectious "sunny side of everything" made the journey that much easier.

———

WE ALSO WANT to thank Dr. Donna Vallone and Dr. Ilene Cohen for their invaluable advice, consultation, and help in evaluating our Grit Quiz.

They say you can't judge a book by its cover, but the right cover has the power to convey the very essence and excitement of a book. Karl Turkel and Michael Nagin, art director at the Crown Publishing Group, thank you for the brilliant and breakthrough design that graces the cover of *Grit to Great.*

A very warm thank-you to everyone who started the Kaplan Thaler Group with us: Lisa Bifulco, Gerry Killeen, Laurie Garnier, Rob Snyder, Andy Landorf, Whitney Pillsbury, Jason Graff, Sharon Petro, and so many others. Your grit and determination catapulted our small fledgling company into one of America's fastest-growing advertising agencies and inspired so many of the stories in our book.

A very special thank-you to Maurice Levy, CEO of the Publicis Groupe; Arthur Sadoun, CEO of Publicis Worldwide; Andrew Bruce, CEO of Publicis North America; Kevin Sweeney, CFO of Publicis North America; as well as Lizzie Dewhurst, the Global Communications Director at Publicis Worldwide. Your support and enthusiasm for our book are so very deeply appreciated. And kudos to the team at Publicis Kaplan Thaler in New York for their time and efforts in helping us edit, shoot, and produce so many of the communications used to promote our book: Lisa Bifulco, head of integrated production; and Marc Lagana, our videographer and consummate editor. And a thank-you as well to all the talented designers at Prodigious.

An enthusiastic thank-you to the entire staff at Truth Initiative (formerly Legacy) for your support and inspiration. You are all a daily reminder of the life-saving impact of grit. And special thanks to Lindsey Kozberg, chief communications officer; and Bill Furmanski for your support and help in bringing *Grit to Great*'s message to life for the nonprofit community. We also want to express our very grateful appreciation to *Truth Initiative*'s entire board of directors and staff for your dedication and commitment to the enduring principles of grit. You provide us all with daily examples of the change we can effect in the world when we apply guts, resilience, initiative, and tenacity.

A very special thanks to our tireless assistants, Fran Marzano; Paula Kostiuk; as well as Gale Duval, manager for board relations; for always being there when we needed them, even if the hours ran late. All of you exemplify the true meaning of grit, and it is so deeply appreciated. And a special thank-you to Josie Forde, who was there at the beginning and has shown her own grit in launching her new career.

Through the many long months of writing and researching, we have been fortunate to uncover myriad insights, information, and stories from friends, clients, colleagues, and relatives, each of whom has helped us to illustrate the transformative power of grit: Meghan Dunn, Bob Deutsch, Steve Sadove, Richard Turere, Marilyn and Seymour Wilensky, Marvin and Bertha Kaplan, the team at Aflac Insurance, Wendy Thomas, Dave Thomas, Clarence Nicodemus, Angela Duckworth, Dean Stamoulis, Mark Murphy, James Patterson, Marin Alsop, Lou and Fabiano Caruana, Nik Wallenda, Lee Yoon-Hye, Jason Comely, Bob Mankoff, Sabrina Farmer, Mike Moore, Mike Lewis, John Mack, Michael Motto, Eleanor Longden, Edith Weill, Nicole Kahn, Malvern Hoyt, David Hoyt, Abe Fichtenbaum, Isabel Ament, Naomi Ament, Ona Robinson, Evelyn Wynn-Dixon, Danny Flamberg, Carol Dweck, Haskell Wexler, Sheldon Yellen, Genevieve Damaschi, Manning Rubin, Lawrence Katz, Marc Freedman, Navyn Salem, Leticia Van de Putte, Trevor Houser, Brian Bob, Ashley Johnson, Margrét Pála Ólafsdóttir, Francine LeFrak, Cindy Ayers-Elliott, Todd Golub, Sid Lerner, Joel Kweskin, and the selfless team of leaders at New York City's Covenant House.

And, of course, our heartfelt thanks to our respective families:

To MY WONDERFUL husband, Kenneth Koval, who, through all these years, has never failed to be a source of inspiration, as well as my biggest fan. And to my beautiful and talented daughter, Melissa Koval: you are an extraordinary and brilliant woman and I am so very proud of you.

To my husband, Fred Thaler, for being my biggest advocate, my best friend, and the love of my life. To our children, Emily and Michael, for bringing such joy into our lives. You never cease to amaze and delight us with your amazing talents and intelligence.

To everyone we have included in these pages, and to the

many people who have touched our lives with their tenacity, initiative, and resilience, we thank you for being such a source of inspiration for *Grit to Great*.

We hope our book inspires you to use your grit to turn your dreams into a brilliant and dazzling reality. Enjoy the journey and never give up.

Linda Kaplan Thaler & Robin Koval

Index

About the Authors

Advertising Hall of Fame luminary **Linda Kaplan Thaler** is the creative force behind many of the industry's most famous campaigns, including the hilarious Aflac Duck, Kodak Moments, and the daring "Yes! Yes! Yes!" for Herbal Essences. Much of her work has become part of the pop culture landscape, including "I'm a Toys 'R' Us Kid," America's longest-running jingle. Linda has also worked on presidential campaigns for Bill Clinton and Hillary Clinton.

Linda is cofounder and former CEO of the Kaplan Thaler Group, which she grew from a small start-up in her brownstone to a billion-dollar agency working with Procter & Gamble, Pfizer, and Wendy's, to name a few. Following its integration with Publicis Worldwide, she became chairman of the agency's flagship office, Publicis Kaplan Thaler.

Linda is also a bestselling author and television personality, appearing on *The Apprentice,* CNN, the *Today* show, and *Good Morning America,* and as host of the Oxygen series *Making It Big*. All her collaborations with coauthor Robin

Koval have become bestsellers: *The Power of Nice, The Power of Small,* and *Bang! Getting Your Message Heard in a Noisy World.*

Linda's talents have earned her the prestigious Matrix Award, the Muse award, and the Advertising Woman of the Year award, and she is recognized as one of *Advertising Age*'s "Most Influential Women in Advertising."

Robin Koval is CEO and president of the Truth Initiative, the national public health foundation dedicated to achieving a culture where all youth and young adults reject tobacco.

A leader in the world of advertising and marketing, Koval became CEO and president of the Truth Initiative in 2013. She has since relaunched the organization's award-winning and lifesaving **truth**® youth tobacco-prevention campaign, named by *Ad Age* as one of the top campaigns of the century.

Koval is cofounder and former president of the Kaplan Thaler Group, which she grew from a fledgling start-up in 1997 to a billion-dollar agency working with Procter & Gamble, Pfizer, Citi, Aflac, and other cherished brands. She led the agency's integration with Publicis and served as CEO of Publicis Kaplan Thaler, New York's fifth largest advertising agency.

She is coauthor of three other bestselling books: *The Power of Nice, The Power of Small, and Bang! Getting Your Message Heard in a Noisy World.*

A highly awarded and sought-after expert on advertising, media, youth culture, and tobacco control, Koval regularly appears on television, contributes commentary to print and online outlets, and speaks at conferences and colloquia for business, government, and media audiences.

Transform how you live and work with these powerful bestsellers from Linda Kaplan Thaler and Robin Koval

It pays to be nice. Filled with inspiration and suggestions on how to supercharge your career and expand your reach in the workplace, these real-life stories will transform how you live and work.

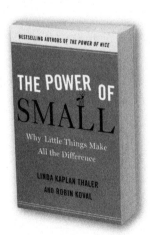

Contrary to the popular adage, you should sweat the small stuff. After all, if you can't take care of the small details, how can you be counted on to deliver when it really matters?

CROWN
BUSINESS
NEW YORK